Patricia Highsmith

Twayne's United States Authors Series

Frank Day, Editor

Clemson University

TUSAS 683

PATRICIA HIGHSMITH
Photo by Jerry Bauer.

Patricia Highsmith

Russell Harrison

Minsk State Linguistic University

Twayne Publishers
An Imprint of Simon & Schuster Macmillan
New York

Prentice Hall International
London • Mexico City • New Delhi • Singapore • Sydney • Toronto

Twayne's United States Authors Series No. 683

Patricia Highsmith
Russell Harrison

Twayne Publishers
An Imprint of Simon & Schuster Macmillan
1633 Broadway
New York, NY 10019

Library of Congress Cataloging-in-Publication Data

Harrison, Russell, 1944–
    Patricia Highsmith / Russell Harrison.
        p.   cm. — (Twayne's United States authors series ; TUSAS 683)
    Includes bibliographical references (p.) and index.
    ISBN 0-8057-4566-1 (alk. paper)
    1. Highsmith, Patricia, 1921–1995—Criticism and interpretation.
2. Women and literature—United States—History—20th century.
3. Detective and mystery stories, American—History and criticism.
4. Psychological fiction, American—History and criticism.
5. Existentialism in literature.   6. Crime in literature.
I. Title.   II. Series.
PS3558.I366Z69   1997
813'.54—dc21   97-18792
                                                                              CIP

10 9 8 7 6 5 4 3 2

For Emma Tompkins Harrison
and
in memory of Milton Harrison,
1907–1968

Thus I am responsible for the existence of my possessions in the human order. Through ownership I raise them up to a certain type of functional being. . . . I draw the collection of my surroundings into being along with myself. If they are taken from me, they die as my arm would die if it were severed from me.

Sartre, *Being and Nothingness*

What boredom and despair those objects we know only too well possess. They play a role in human existence as important as people.

Paul Nizan, *Aden-Arabie*

Contents

Preface

Patricia Highsmith's fiction presents the critic with one of the most unusual bodies of work in postwar American literature. For a long time, her work was, in the United States, viewed as crime or suspense fiction. This was not a valid categorization, however, although Highsmith's work does bear some similarities to those genres. Indeed, at the beginning of her career, Highsmith had viewed herself as simply a novelist (and in France and Germany she has always been regarded as such).[1] Although reviewers occasionally granted her novels the status of serious (as opposed to formula) fiction, it was not until the 1980s that bookstores began to shelve her novels in the literature section rather than in the mystery section.[2] This study endorses that retail classification and makes no attempt to situate her work in either the detective or suspense fiction categories.

Critics who have viewed Highsmith as a serious novelist have focused on her representation and analysis of the emotions, primarily guilt. Although this approach to her work is more accurate (indeed, Highsmith's early work bears the influence of the postwar existentialism of Sartre and Camus, as well as of certain protoexistentialist writers such as Dostoyevsky and Gide), a view of Highsmith as a subtle analyst of human emotions misses the mark. Such a response sees her treatment of guilt and analysis of motivation in general as psychologically realistic, as if she were developing the mode of psychological analysis associated with writers such as Austen, James, or Proust. However, notwithstanding Highsmith's seemingly conventional prose style, the mental world of her protagonists does not resemble that of literary realism. While no literary world truly exists, no matter how many "realistic" and "right" details it exhibits, the rhetoric of the realist writer aims at establishing between the narrator and the reader the fiction that the author is attempting to describe a real world. Highsmith's narrator does not do this. The reader may be confused by the "wealth" of detail that this commodity-obsessed narrator presents, as well as by the mundane middle-class facade her characters show. Psychological realism, however, plays a minor role. More significant is her ability to create in readers states of extreme psychological tension unlike anything produced by her contemporaries.

A moment ago I referred to a "commodity-obsessed narrator." One of the most striking aspects of Highsmith's novels, something that critics have rarely noted (and then only as a stylistic element—an attention to detail), is the obsession with the material aspects of life, for the most part in the form of consumer goods. This fixation is a marked and revealing feature of her texts that both creates and reflects the objectified quality of her characters' lives as it both creates and reflects their strangely dissociated personalities. Ultimately this "flight into objects" is a fear of a loss of control. Repressed drives are deflected onto possessions the characters can control. Commodities are the perfect focus for this cathexis because it is their essence to be possessed. The power that such objects possess in Highsmith's novels derives from their role as the repository of emotions whose "correct" object lies elsewhere. It is the power of suppression and displacement.

There is also a political dimension to Highsmith's fiction that, especially in the earlier novels, is not immediately apparent. Because this displacement mimics the displacement the cold war effected in American life—especially in the 1950s and the early 1960s—it is more profound and harder to see. As sex is everywhere in Highsmith's novels, though not necessarily treated directly, so the political is similarly pervasive, if even more invisible. Although her novels from the late 1960s on dealt more directly with social and political change in the United States, the earlier novels were also the products of (the suppression of) politics that constituted cold-war America. This is most clearly the case in the novels I treat in chapter 3—*Deep Water* (1957), *This Sweet Sickness* (1960), and *The Cry of the Owl* (1962). In these novels, the obsessive and quasi-maniacal "individualism" of protagonists frozen in isolated small-town or exurban American comfort combines with their lives devoted to work and their obsessions to produce a world apparently typical and yet mostly untouched by national and international events. Hence, it comes as no surprise that the politics of the era surface in convoluted and oblique ways.

In light of what I have just suggested concerning the displacements and suppressions of Highsmith's fiction, my interpretations necessarily involve reading "against the grain." This is not, however, to dismiss the manifest content as irrelevant or unimportant. When, for example, in *Edith's Diary* (1977), Highsmith wrote a novel about a divorced woman forced to come to terms with her position in society and concerned to establish her independence, this feminist aspect of the book cannot be ignored. Highsmith is no social novelist, but like any novelist of consequence, she reflects her times willy-nilly. Long ago Georg Lukács pointed out that a novel's tendency may directly contradict the professed political or social views of its author (his favorite example was Balzac, a confirmed monarchical reactionary who faithfully represented the rising bourgeoisie as the unstoppable wave of the future), and Highsmith represents an especially tricky example of this disjunction.

One final caveat should be noted. When Patricia Highsmith died in February 1995, the *New York Times*, in an early edition of its obituary, identified the deceased as "Mrs. Ripley," confusing her with the hero of Highsmith's series of novels devoted to Tom Ripley. The obituary went on to say that Highsmith's "tales . . . were often explorations of her own obsessions."[3] Such identification of Highsmith and her writing is not useful. My study discusses her texts, and while reference to her biography is occasionally helpful, it does not form the basis of my analysis. Indeed, when I speak of "Highsmith," it is most often a convenient shorthand in no way denoting or implying the historical individual. Rather, it designates the "implied author" whose image we have in mind when, as readers, we imagine the creator of these texts.

Acknowledgments

I would like especially to thank Bettina Berch for having read and made detailed comments on several chapters and for having provided me with useful secondary material. I would also like to thank David Friedkin, George Greaney, and Nancy Kennedy for having read parts of the manuscript and for their helpful suggestions. I also want to thank Neil Donahue for his unerringly appropriate professional advice.

I want to acknowledge the aid of and thank Charles Latimer and Kate Skattebol, friends of Patricia Highsmith's, who provided me with useful and otherwise unobtainable biographical material.

Finally, I want to thank Frank Day and Anne Davidson for their helpful and timely editorial assistance.

Chronology

1921 Mary Patricia Highsmith born January 19 in Fort Worth, Texas, the only child of Jay Bernard Plangman and Mary Coates. Her parents divorce shortly after she is born.

1927 Moves to New York to live with her mother and her stepfather, Stanley Highsmith.

1933 Spends a year in Fort Worth and sees her father for the first time.

1938 Graduates from Julia Richman High School in Manhattan.

1942 B.A. degree from Barnard College. Studies literature and zoology.

1944 Legally adopted by Stanley Highsmith.

1945 Publishes first short story, "The Heroine," in *Harper's Bazaar*.

1948 Accepted at Yaddo artists' colony through the help of Truman Capote. (Much of *Strangers on a Train* was written at Yaddo.)

1950 *Strangers on a Train* is published. Highsmith receives $6,800 for the film rights from Alfred Hitchcock. Raymond Chandler and Czenzi Ormonde write the screenplay.

1952 *The Price of Salt* is published under the name of Claire Morgan by Coward McCann after having been rejected by Harper and Brothers. Published the next year in paperback, it sells nearly 1,000,000 copies.

1955 *The Talented Mr. Ripley*.

1957 *Deep Water*. Highsmith is awarded the Edgar Allan Poe Scroll from the Mystery Writers of America and the Grand Prix de Litterature Policière for *The Talented Mr. Ripley*.

1960 *This Sweet Sickness*.

1961   *The Talented Mr. Ripley* filmed by René Clément as *Plein Soleil (Purple Noon)*.

1962   *The Cry of the Owl*.

1963   Moves to England, first to Aldeburgh, then to the Suffolk village of Earl Soham from 1964 to 1966.

1967   Moves to France, first to Montmachoux, near Fontainebleau, later to Moncourt, also near Fontainebleau.

1972   *A Dog's Ransom*.

1977   *Edith's Diary* published by Simon and Schuster (after having been rejected by Knopf).

1982   Moves to Aurigeno, near Locarno (Ticino) in Italian Switzerland.

1986   *Found in the Street*.

1988   Moves to Tegna, also near Locarno.

1991   *Ripley under Water*. *The Price of Salt* reprinted under the author's name.

1995   *Small g: A Summer Idyll*, Highsmith's last novel, is published in England, France, and Germany. It is rejected by Knopf in the United States. Dies February 4 from a combination of lung cancer and aplastic anemia. Leaves estate of approximately $5,000,000.

Chapter One

Introduction

Biography

Patricia Highsmith was born on January 19, 1921, in Fort Worth, Texas, the only child of Jay Bernard Plangman and Mary Coates. Her mother's family, English-Scots by descent, came from Alabama; her father's family, of German descent, had been in Texas for several generations. Highsmith's parents separated five months before her birth and divorced "for reasons which [she was] never . . . able to understand" shortly after she was born.[1] Highsmith did not meet her father until she was 12 and was "more or less raised" by her grandmother in Texas until the age of 6.[2] Indeed, she has said that her grandmother was the only person from whom she experienced real tenderness: "I loved her. I would have gladly remained with her. Mama was against it. Something went to pieces in me when I left my grandmother. I totally withdrew into myself."[3] At age six she moved with her mother, a commercial artist who worked as a fashion illustrator for *Women's Wear Daily*, and her stepfather, Stanley Highsmith, an advertising illustrator (whom her mother married when Highsmith was three), to New York City. Her mother's second marriage, however, was not successful. According to Highsmith her mother often quarreled with her stepfather, and they moved frequently in New York. Her mother and stepfather separated when Highsmith was 12, again when she was 16, and again when she was 19 (Maerker, 149).

Hence, Highsmith's childhood and adolescence do not appear to have been happy, nor, indeed, does her prenatal existence. According to Highsmith, her mother tried to abort the fetus: "She really tried to get rid of it—she told me—I didn't mind. She said, 'It's funny you adore the smell of turpentine, Pat.' Because she drank turpentine before I was born trying to have a miscarriage. I didn't mind one bit."[4] "Why don't I love my mother?" Highsmith once asked in an interview. "First, because she made my childhood a little hell. Second, because she herself never loved anyone, neither my father, my stepfather, nor me" (Loriot, 29).

Whereas some might see a correlation between her biography and her fiction, Highsmith rejected such a connection: "I must say I mistrust writers who use their family because I think they're not imaginative. . . . Some dramatic things happened in my family, but I wouldn't dream of writing about them" (Dupont, 64). After Julia Richman High School, Highsmith attended Barnard College (graduating in 1942). She had begun writing stories at age 16 and continued doing so at Barnard, where she wrote "The Heroine," a story considered "too horrifying" to publish in the college magazine (Wakeman, n.p.). It was later published in *Harper's Bazaar* and was also included in the *O. Henry Prize Stories of 1946*. In 1948 Truman Capote (a writer she admired) helped her get into Yaddo, an artists' colony in upstate New York, where she worked on *Strangers on a Train*. This, her third novel (though the first to be published), was rejected six times before finally finding a publisher. She received $6,800 for the film and stage rights, and when the screenplay was filmed by Alfred Hitchcock, it launched her career.

After graduating from Barnard, Highsmith lived with her parents in an apartment on Grove Street in Greenwich Village and wrote comic-book scenarios "of the Superman and Batman variety to earn a living" while writing serious fiction in the evenings and on weekends (Wakeman, n.p.). Later, in the 1950s and 1960s, Highsmith traveled a good deal and lived in a variety of places, including Europe for two years in the early 1950s (after a first trip in 1949). While living mostly in Manhattan she also spent a fair amount of time in Mexico, which she had first visited in 1943, and the American Southwest. She moved to Europe for good in 1963, living first in England from 1963 to 1966, then in France from 1967 to 1982, and finally in Switzerland from 1982 till her death in 1995, all the while producing a steady stream of novels and short stories. Although somewhat reclusive, she gave a fair number of interviews over the years and visited the United States with some regularity, sometimes to research a novel. In 1991 she acknowledged her authorship of the lesbian novel *The Price of Salt* (originally published in 1952 under the pseudonym Claire Morgan)—an acknowledgment, as well, that times had changed.

Influences and Themes

As I stated in the preface, this study treats Highsmith simply as a novelist and short-story writer and makes no attempt to analyze her work with respect to such subgenres as crime or suspense fiction. My discussion of Highsmith's work focuses on aspects that elucidate it and allow us to situate it historically. These are (1) its relationship to and use of certain elements of the existentialism of Sartre and Camus (and of such existentialist precursors as Dostoyevsky and Gide); (2) the various, and sometimes oblique, ways her fiction reflects its sociohistorical moment, from the cold war of the late 1940s and 1950s, through its increasing politicization in the late 1960s and 1970s, to the gay and lesbian novels (and the acknowledgment of *The Price of Salt*) of her last decade; (3) the depiction of interpersonal relationships and of the family; and (4) the role that objects, most often in the form of commodities, play in the lives of her characters and, in certain instances, in the language of the texts themselves. The rest of this chapter develops these categories as the background for an analysis of her work.

French Existentialism

No recent philosophical movement has had anything like the impact on American literature that the existentialism of Sartre and Camus did in roughly the decade and a half following the end of World War II. A brief look at the historical context of existentialism's rise will illuminate the appeal it held for many writers, including Highsmith. In its idealist emphasis on the isolated individual subject, existentialism embodied a reaction against the increasingly circumscribed role that the various nineteenth-century determinisms granted the individual as well as against the severe limitations placed on the individual in the 1930s and during World War II. As one scholar noted, there was a "decline of rationality in bourgeois ideology and society, under the impact of structural crisis, fascism, the authoritarian state and monopoly capitalism."[5] The apparently ineluctable horrors of the two world wars and the brutal economic conditions of the 1930s, against which individuals, tossed about by forces beyond their control, could do little to affect their fate, seemed indeed to produce a situation in which even to choose was a kind of absurdity. Such a situation called forth in reaction—and almost as a last gasp—the existentialist insistence on the individual's freedom. Sartre argued that even under extreme physical duress, indeed, torture, one has a choice: "No matter what resistance the victim has offered, no matter how long he has waited before begging for mercy, he would have been able despite all to wait ten minutes, one minute, one second longer. He has *determined* the moment at which the pain became unbearable. The proof is that he will live out his abjuration in remorse and shame. Thus he is entirely responsible for it."[6] This responsibility might even be realized in bad faith: "We can choose ourselves as fleeing, inapprehensible, as indecisive, etc." (Sartre, 607). No matter, the choice remains ours.

More directly influential than Sartre because of its expression in more accessible forms was the existentialism of Albert Camus. In his novels and essays, Camus derived the concept of the absurd from the impossibility of man's knowing any transcendent meaning, of "reduc[ing] this world to a rational and reasonable principle."[7] The meaninglessness of any "totalizing" view of reality (to use a term of more recent provenance), whether religious, political, or philosophical, led to a pluralizing of meaning: no choice was inherently more rational than any other. To be sure, it was still necessary to choose, but because no choice was transcendentally justified, all choices were equally (ir)rational. The literary antecedents of such a worldview were clear in such works as Dostoyevsky's *Notes from Underground* (1863), whose narrator opined that "a man . . . always and everywhere likes to act as he chooses, and not at all according to the dictates of reason and self-interest," and in Gide's *Lafcadio's Adventures* (*Les caves du Vatican* [1914]), which adumbrated a quasi-aleatory view of human motivation. Both texts echo clearly in Highsmith's earlier novels.[8] Indeed, she has claimed Dostoyevsky as her favorite author.

This view of the absurdity of choice—yet its necessity—and the privileging of the irrational and even motiveless in human behavior underlay much of Highsmith's fiction of the 1950s. Indeed, Charles Bruno's confession to Guy Haines in *Strangers on a Train* that he had committed a burglary and "taken just what he didn't want" is almost too close a fit to Gide's protoexistentialist Lafcadio. But it is just this undercurrent of the absurd and the irrational that Highsmith proceeded to domesticate (both literally and figuratively) in the series of novels that followed, most clearly in *Deep Water* (1957) and *This Sweet Sickness* (1960). This influence explains one of the most striking aspects of Highsmith's novels, which extended beyond her first decade as a novelist: the often irrational behavior of her characters. As one critic noted: "Readers become irritated with her characters seeing ways in which circumstances could have been avoided, loopholes sought and danger eluded."[9] Why doesn't Guy Haines go to the police in *Strangers on a Train*? Why does Walter Stackhouse seek out Melchior Kimmel in *The Blunderer*? Why does Rydal Keener help Chester McFarland, a stranger, dispose of the body of a dead policeman in *Two Faces of January*? Such moments in Highsmith's novels are meant to suggest not just the motiveless aspect of human behavior but, more important, her characters' freedom. In this, Highsmith shared in the existentialist moment of postwar American literature.

Graham Greene, in the most frequently cited essay on Highsmith, wrote that "[h]er characters are irrational and they leap to life in the very lack of reason; suddenly we realize how unbelievably rational most fictional characters are."[10] But Highsmith was not alone in her positive stance toward the irrational. When confronted by the irrational behavior of Highsmith's characters, we are reminded of this aspect of modernist literature (Greene included) generally. One need go no further, for example, than Saul Bellow's 1947 novel *The Victim* (another novel indebted to existentialism) to become aware of irrational behavior that would be perfectly "appropriate" in a Highsmith novel of the following decade. It is perhaps more accurate to say that such irrationality (re)emphasizes the constructed nature of fictional reality and, some might say, of reality itself.

Whereas the irrationality of Highsmith's characters was an attempt to assert their freedom and their humanity, the exaggerated nature of their behavior might suggest a reaction against a determination felt as equally strong. By the late 1950s, Highsmith's existentialists suffered a sea change. Their penchant for choosing—in Sartre's terms, their involvement in their "project"—became "privatized." That is, the thrust of what in Sartre and Camus had been a political response to the increasingly brutal and determining forces of history, and in *Strangers on a Train* and *The Talented Mr. Ripley* still possessed a philosophical force, now became increasingly idiosyncratic. The "project" was trivialized into a hobby or an obsession, whether manifested in Vic Van Allen's snails or David Kelsey's ideal house. The lack of historical context led to existentialism's being turned on its head. Choice pushed in extremis became obsession, and thus the very opposite of choice, most vividly expressed through the character of David Kelsey in *This Sweet Sickness*. The upshot is that Highsmith's characters of the decade's end choose projects that they cannot "surpass." Indeed, their "finitude was the condition of their freedom" (Sartre, 432). They did, however, continue to choose existing and ceasing to exist through that choice. But with *The Cry of the Owl* (1962) another shift occurred, via a shadowy subtext hinting at small-town McCarthyism, which suggests a response to the political witch-hunts of the 1950s. Gradually thereafter, politics came to assume a more conscious presence in her novels as the programmatic existentialism of her protagonists diminished.

Existentialism was an idealist response to the horrors of the 1930s and the worse horrors of World War II and the extermination camps, a statement that there was a way out for a humanity subject to seemingly inexorable and determining historical forces.[11] It performed a similar function in Highsmith's fiction. Reacting against the literature of the 1930s, especially that which depicted people as overwhelmingly determined by their circumstances, Highsmith's fiction pushed "choice" to a solipsistic extreme.[12] In fact, this is one reason she sets the three key novels in this period in small towns where the anonymous and often overwhelming forces of modernity appear less powerful and her characters' freedom of action correspondingly greater. One can hardly imagine David Kelsey setting up his fantasized life with Annabelle Stanton in a Manhattan apartment.

One last aspect of Highsmith's novels can fruitfully be discussed in the context of her debt to existentialism. Related to the issues of choice and the irrational, but not subsumed by them, this aspect can be categorized as "irritation" and reflects Highsmith's tendency to personalize what had been political or social in origin. As Klein noted, often enough this irritation arises in the reader's struggle to escape identification with the passive protagonists and the enormous self-control they must exercise. Why doesn't Guy Haines just refuse Bruno's demands? Why doesn't Robert Forester say enough is enough to his ex-wife Nickie, or Vic Van Allen to Melinda's infidelities? The power such situations exert on the reader is surprising and derives from the frustration we feel between our "natural" desire for the character to act, to assert himself, and our recognition that one doesn't give in to one's emotions in this way. Here Highsmith most closely replicates the responses that Kafka's texts produce. Highsmith's frustrated characters (and readers) may legitimately be compared to Kafka's famously frustrated K's. Yet, although the feeling is the same, the cause differs significantly. Kafka's protagonists are caught in a web of bureaucratic control, Highsmith's in private and self-imposed constraints. In *The Trial* and *The Castle,* the state bureaucracy confronts the protagonist. In Highsmith's fiction, the threat always comes from another individual, whether family member, boss, or stranger. The frustrations of Kafka's stories and novels were the product of society, responses to the increasing bureaucratic condition of modern social life, to the objective world, and, in the last analysis, to history. Highsmith, too, reflects her times, but in a much more mediated manner.

By the late 1950s and the early 1960s, Highsmith's characters have reversed Camus's adjuration to live "without appeal." The projects of

Charles Bruno and Tom Ripley have devolved into the obsessive irrationality of David Kelsey and the hypertrophied and obsessive rationality of Robert Forester. But with Forester's situation in *The Cry of the Owl* (1962), Highsmith's work begins to acknowledge the role society plays in the lives of her characters.

The Social and the Political Aspect of Highsmith's Novels

Much of Highsmith's work might seem to resist a political reading. Yet there are a number of indications that such an analysis is appropriate. The dilemma with which one is faced is nicely reflected in the dedication of her 1983 novel, *People Who Knock on the Door*:

> To the courage of the Palestinian people and their leaders in the struggle
> to regain a part of their homeland.
>   This book has nothing to do with their problem.

Such a dedication has a political resonance, though it requires elaboration. There is an apologetic tone to the last sentence, as if the author felt the charge of bad faith in that her novel *should* have something to do with "their" problem. But it also suggests that the author accepts a division between the politics of the writer and what she writes. Eight years later, Highsmith dedicated *Ripley under Water* "To the dead and the dying among the Intifadah and the Kurds, to those who fight aggression in whatever land, and stand up not only to be counted but to be shot." Here the dedicatees are a much expanded group, the book is actually dedicated to them rather than a quality they possess, and there is no hint of bad faith. I cite these dedications in part to show that Highsmith herself possessed a political awareness but also to suggest possible complications in this awareness as the novels express it.

Highsmith's earliest novels are the least concerned with politics. Only with the increasing importance given to society through the prominence of the small-town societies in *Deep Water, This Sweet Sickness,* and *The Cry of the Owl* do we sense that her characters inhabit a social world. Indeed, in chapter 3, my interpretation of *The Cry of the Owl* suggests that in this novel the political is close to breaking through to the surface. But it is in *The Glass Cell* that we begin to see an awareness of political struggle. In the novel, Philip Carter, unjustly convicted of embezzlement, is imprisoned for six years. The climax of his years in jail occurs as he takes part in a riot over unjust prison regulations (the only depiction of any collective political action in Highsmith's novels). Although the cause of the prisoners' outbreak verges on trivializing their situation, the fact that such a collective action occurs represents an important change in her novels.[13]

In roughly the second half of her career (beginning with *The Tremor of Forgery* [1969]), and especially in her novels of the 1970s, the sociopolitical content becomes more overt, reflecting the increasingly dynamic political scene in the United States from the rise of the counterculture and the antiestablishment "threat" of the 1960s and early 1970s, reflected in *A Dog's Ransom* (1972), the only novel in which the state plays a prominent role, through the Friedanesque feminism of *Edith's Diary* (1977), to the gay and lesbian fiction of her last decade. What this synopsis suggests is that Highsmith's novels, as well as her stories, have an important and increasingly manifest political content.

Closely related to—at times inseparable from—the political aspect of the novels is the social world they depict. It is, almost without exception, a middle-class world composed of the free professions: architects, lawyers, engineers, and scientists, successful small businesspeople and what we might term creative technocrats: TV scriptwriters, stage designers, editors, journalists, and commercial artists. In not one of her novels does the protagonist work for a large corporation or a large government bureaucracy (if one excepts Tom Ripley's few months with the IRS). In light of the fact that her novels are products of the second half of the twentieth century, by which time, with the entrenchment of monopoly capitalism and the welfare state, the large corporation and government had long since become the primary employers in the U.S. economy, Highsmith's narrow focus on an increasingly powerless and diminishing stratum produces a skewed picture of American social life. While her characters are often enough prisoners of their individual obsessions, the other side of this coin is the unusual freedom their jobs allow them. Indeed, the intense horror of subordinating their lives to the demands of a large organization is nowhere more tellingly expressed than in Anne Faulkner's response (in *Strangers on a Train*) to Guy Haines's mention of the possibility of his going to work for an architectural partnership, "You mean for a firm?" where one catches the note of horror in her voice at this prospective loss of independence.

Another indication, or token, of her characters' freedom is the independent income or inherited wealth that runs like a red thread through their finances. From the oddly denominated checks that Tom Ripley's aunt sends him, through Vic Van Allen's income of $40,000 a year (in

Deep Water), and Philip Carter's inheritance of "about one hundred and twenty-five thousand dollars from his Aunt Martha" (in *The Glass Cell*), or Sydney Bartleby's $100 a month "from some stocks an uncle in America had bequeathed him" (in *A Suspension of Mercy*), through Kenneth Rowajinski's disability pension of $260 a month (in *A Dog's Ransom*) and the free apartment provided Natalia and Jack Sutherland (in *Found in the Street*), and culminating in Luisa Zimmermann's inheritance of a six-figure amount (albeit in Swiss francs) in Highsmith's last novel, *Small g,* her characters rarely have to rely solely on the salary, let alone the wage. Although the amount varies and at times borders on the inconsequential, it is still an important mark of the characters' independent status, something the author feels important to indicate. Equally interesting, and springing from the same cause, is the failure of any of Highsmith's characters to accumulate wealth (other than through inheritance or theft).[14] Their financial position remains pretty much the same at the end of the novel as it was at the beginning, attesting to the static social world that they inhabit.

The Family

Noëlle Loriot once asked Highsmith whether she had ever made an attempt to live with someone. "Indeed," said Highsmith, "but it was catastrophic. Basically everything goes back to my childhood. My parents' apartment was small, so I had to sleep in the living room. I would have had to be deaf not to have heard the cutting words with which my mother tormented my stepfather. This life plagued by marital discord finally traumatized me. So, the pleasures of family life, no, thanks" (Loriot, 24). Indeed, in her work, it is rare to find a good word said for the family.

One might be tempted to accept Highsmith's self-analysis (ignoring, for the moment, her denial of any relationship between her life and her subject matter) as explanation for the negative depiction of the family and for the problems her characters have relating to one another. Yet although the only fortunate romantic pairings in her novels are those of Therese Belivet and Carol Auld in *The Price of Salt* and Tom and Heloise Ripley in the later Ripley novels, what is of more moment is the extent to which her characters seem torn between intense interpersonal strife and a compulsion to find a modus vivendi with one another. From the Stackhouses' troubled marriage in *The Blunderer* and Vic and Melinda Van Allen's intense isolation à deux in *Deep Water*, through Robert

Forester's agonizing ambivalence over his relationship with Jenny Thierolf in *The Cry of the Owl,* to the delicate arrangement of Jack and Natalia Sutherland in *Found in the Street,* we have not only a detailed depiction of the problematic nature of marriage but also the sense that on some level Highsmith's characters clearly need an other. It is a strategy of mutual assured destruction writ small: if anyone launches an attack, there will be immediate and overwhelming retaliation, and indeed the couples are often at the brink. But—as was true of the United States and the Soviet Union—they remain intensely engaged with one another. Moreover, although the reality may be unpleasant, as in Wes and Laura Carpenter's marriage in *This Sweet Sickness,* there is always the fantasy of the ideal: there, David Kelsey's fantasy marriage with Annabelle Stanton.

With rare exceptions (most notably the Van Allens in *Deep Water*), Highsmith's couples do not reproduce. There is a kind of *horror pleni* at the idea of the complete nuclear family. Moreover, not only are children virtually vanquished from the novels, but so are parents. By this I mean that Highsmith's protagonists are rarely placed in relation to their own parents. This lacuna contributes to one of the most striking tropes in the novels. I noted that many of her characters are provided with independent incomes or inherited wealth; however, this money never derives from a biological parent. The consistency with which this is the case suggests the strength of the dynamic. In *The Blunderer,* Walter Stackhouse lives in a house given to his wife by her mother; an aunt sends Tom Ripley his checks; a grandfather wills Vic Van Allen his $40,000 a year; an aunt leaves Philip Carter $125,000; an uncle gives Sydney Bartleby $125 a month; an aunt gives Jack and Natalia Sutherland their apartment; and Luisa Zimmermann inherits a substantial sum from her late boss, Renate Hagnauer.

Parents and children are best avoided altogether. The ramifications of this phenomenon are far-reaching and most notably affect the role sex plays in the novels. Highsmith once said that she was embarrassed by sex scenes in movies and closed her eyes when they appeared on the screen (Dupont, 66). With the notable exception of the sexual relations of Carol and Therese in *The Price of Salt,* the novels, as it were, shut their eyes when sex appears, if ever so dimly, on the horizon. It is hard to recall in all the fiction a scene of two bodies in sexual contact. Such sex as does exist occurs offstage. One could not fault Highsmith for not wanting to include such scenes in her novels; for all the freedom that writers have had in this area for the last three decades, it is still an area

that many treat gingerly. What makes the area problematic in Highsmith is her obvious desire to include the sexual in her characters' lives
while at the same time clearly operating under self-imposed constraints.
One of the oddest signs of this is that occasionally her characters will
have had sexual intercourse "two or three times" (before the novel
begins) and then decided to refrain from it.[15] It is as if sex is something
unpleasant that has to be gotten out of the way, like a rabies shot.

Yet this negative portrayal of the family is limited to the *biological*
family and the sexual relationship that produces it. Highsmith sometimes constructs ersatz families that she portrays quite positively: for
example, in *A Dog's Ransom,* Ed and Greta Reynolds act as fond foster
parents to Clarence Duhamell, much as the kindly Dr. Knot functions
as a substitute father for Robert Forester in *The Cry of the Owl* (though he
gets shot for his efforts). Indeed, in Highsmith's last novel, *Small g,* the
habitués of the bar around which that novel centers form a kind of
extended family, viewed, as the subtitle of the novel suggests, in an idyl-
lic light. And we should also note that sex, when it cannot result in pro-
creation, as in *The Price of Salt,* is presented with a positiveness verging
on sentimentality.

Those Not So Obscure Objects of Desire: Objects

If Highsmith's texts reveal a profound ambivalence in how they treat
relationships between people, no such conflict appears in either the
characters' or the text's relation to commodities, usually consumer
goods.[16] Whether in fussy descriptive details such as the following
example from *The Tremor of Forgery,* "She was in a loose white coat, white
shoes, carrying a big colorful pocketbook and a sack which looked like
two bottles of something," or in a character's conscious privileging of
objects as in Tom Ripley's *jouissance* at the "spanking tautness" of the
package nets on the Paris-Rome train or Vic Van Allen's ecstatic reaction
to the three Brooks Brothers sweaters Melinda has given him as a birthday present, the role of commodities in the form of consumer goods cannot be overemphasized.[17] This textual characteristic is helpfully eluci-
dated by two different, though mutually rewarding, analyses.

In the classic nineteenth-century novel, detailed objective description
was meant to achieve realism (a word that derives from, interestingly,
not only the Latin *res,* "thing," but a Sanskrit root denoting "property"
or "wealth"). So it was in the great French realists, such as Balzac,
Flaubert, and Zola. "Precision," Theodore Adorno noted in his essay on

Balzac, "simulates extreme closeness to the matter at hand and hence physical presence." But Balzac overestimated the value of the concrete to such an extent that it became an attempt to "conjure up" reality. Adorno, citing Brecht, noted that reality was a process rather than an accumulation of facts. In the end, "Concreteness substitutes for . . . real experience."[18] Surface appearance no longer equated with reality, and no amount of detailed description would help.

Highsmith's details hem the reader in rather than suggest deeper levels of meaning. Here, the added detail does not so much say something about Ina as it hampers the reader's freedom of movement. It shifts the weight of the sentence toward the objects, away from the person. It is by no means the unmarked style, the degree zero of writing, that Highsmith and some critics have suggested; rather, it creates a claustrophobia in which there is no room for anything other than things. Such a dynamic creates texts that are the verbal equivalent of walking through an Ikea showroom, where every foot of floor space is occupied by objects or roomlike clusters of objects, with nothing in bad taste and nothing exceptional; or like those newspaper ads that show model rooms packed with so much furniture that one can hardly imagine moving, let alone living, in such a space.

It is not so much an attempt to describe as to possess reality. What the text accomplishes by its hypertrophied detail is a further appropriation of the object itself. That is, knowing (knowledge being a form of possession) that Ina's sack "looked like two bottles of something" increases our hold on the thing: "To appropriate this object is then to appropriate the world symbolically" (Sartre, 760). The fundamentally alienating aspect of such description is that it leaves no place for the reader. It narrows the reader's field of play, and as Maerker noted, "Her books are written in a manner that one needs little of one's own fantasy when reading them" (152).

Chapter Two

Highsmith in the 1950s

From her first published effort in the form, Patricia Highsmith's novels are strikingly assured in tone and plot and consistent in style. Although the contents of her novels have varied over the years, certain elements, adumbrated in her early novels, remained for a long time an important part of her fiction: significant (homoerotic) relationships between men; a negative, at times verging on the misogynist, cast to her treatment of women; and the irrationality of her characters' actions—all are present here. In this chapter I focus on two novels of the 1950s—Highsmith's formative decade as a novelist—that most clearly represent her concerns at that time, *Strangers on a Train* (1950), and *The Talented Mr. Ripley* (1955). They also happen to be her two best-known novels.

Strangers on a Train (1950)

Strangers on a Train contains all the elements I have noted. It introduces the first of those paired male characters around whose relationship of repulsion and attraction Highsmith's fiction often revolves. Guy Haines, a rising young architect, is traveling on a train from New York City to Metcalf, Texas, to obtain a divorce from his wife, Miriam, in order to be able to marry Anne Faulkner, the woman he now loves. Miriam has been unfaithful to Guy and is now pregnant with another man's child. On the train, Guy meets Charles Anthony Bruno, a young man without job or profession. The son of a wealthy man, Bruno lives with his parents at their Great Neck, New York, estate. Bruno spends much of his time traveling with his mother, of whom he is extremely fond, and as little time as possible with his father, whom he hates and would like to see dead.

In a chance conversation, Bruno surmises that Miriam can create trouble for Guy, not only with respect to his desire to marry Anne but also in his professional life. Guy has submitted a design for a new clubhouse and outbuildings for a prestigious Palm Beach country club and is favored in the competition. But any hint of private scandal might adversely affect his securing the commission and indeed his career in general. Sensing all this, Bruno makes a daring suggestion to Guy: "We murder for each other, see? I kill your wife and you kill my father! We meet on the train, see, and nobody knows we know each other! Perfect alibi! Catch?"[1] Repelled, Guy rejects Bruno's offer, and they part the next day. But Bruno goes ahead and kills Miriam anyway, strangling her at an amusement park outside the small Texas town where she lives (and where Guy grew up). The remainder of the novel revolves around Bruno's attempts to force Guy into fulfilling his end of the "bargain."

Soon after Miriam's murder, Guy receives three letters from Bruno, one of which contains the business card of a Metcalf taxi company. Because Guy had refused Bruno's pact in no uncertain terms and hence, at this point, can in no way be thought culpable for Miriam's death, the question arises as to why he does not immediately go to the police.[2] Guy suspects Bruno but does not do anything, not even telling his fiancée his suspicions because "he could not tell Anne about Bruno until he was sure" and because "he felt it was some sense of personal guilt that he himself could not bear" (*Strangers,* 86). For the moment, Guy decides to let the police trap Bruno. "But as the weeks went by and they didn't, he was plagued by a feeling that he should act himself. What stopped him was both an aversion to accusing a man of murder and a senseless but lingering doubt that Bruno might not be guilty. . . . And yet, he had to admit to himself that he was *sure* Bruno had done it" (*Strangers,* 102). Hence, by not acting as soon as he suspects Bruno, Guy knows he has become complicit. Ultimately, this complicity works against him. Highsmith has stated that she is interested in the effects of guilt on a character. Yet it is often an existential guilt, rather than guilt for a specific act; often, too, it is guilt for a feeling, rather than for an action.[3] Indeed, the extreme guilt that her characters can feel for their thoughts and feelings is the other side of the coin with respect to which other protagonists feel remarkably little guilt for their extreme actions, as for example Tom Ripley and Vic Van Allen for the murders they commit.

In a subsequent conversation that Guy and Bruno have in New York, after Bruno has "appeared out of nowhere, in the middle of the sidewalk," Bruno makes it clear that by not going to the police earlier, Guy has put himself in a suspicious position. When Guy threatens to turn him over to the police, Bruno responds:

> "Why didn't you do that in Metcalf?" Bruno asked with the lowest pink gleam in his eyes, as only he could have asked it, impersonally, sadly, yet with triumph. Oddly, Guy felt his inner voice had asked him the question in the same way.

"Because I wasn't sure enough."

"What do I have to do, make a written statement?"

"I can still turn you over for investigation."

"No, you can't. They've got more on you than on me." Bruno shrugged. (*Strangers,* 109)

Bruno hounds Guy to such a degree, telephoning him at odd moments and unexpectedly accosting him on the street, that Guy begins to consider doing the murder, though at first with the idea of leaving clues that will incriminate Bruno. Finally, in a scene that has something of the supernatural about it (Bruno appears in the night sitting beside Guy's bed—" 'Hi,' Bruno said softly. 'I got in on a passkey. You're ready now, aren't you?' " [*Strangers,* 131]), Guy agrees to the murder.

Nevertheless, Bruno continues to irritate Guy with his unwanted presence, even going so far as to appear at Guy's wedding. He later becomes friendly with Anne, who wants to know him better because she has connected him with Guy's depression, which continues as the murder of Samuel Bruno approaches and worsens afterward. Indeed, while Guy, whose career has been succeeding beyond his fondest dreams (articles have appeared hailing him as the most important young American architect) is away on a dam project in Canada, Bruno has driven up to visit Anne at the Connecticut house designed by Guy. During this visit, Bruno gets so drunk that he has to be put to bed for the night in the guest room.

Guy commits the murder in the vain hope of ridding himself of Bruno once and for all. But even after Guy has murdered Bruno's father, Bruno continues to hound Guy and Anne. One day, Bruno goes sailing with them and two friends on Long Island Sound. Drunk and boisterous, he falls off the boat and drowns, in spite of Guy's efforts to rescue him. The novel does not end there, however. Arthur Gerard, a private investigator retained by Bruno's mother to investigate her husband's murder, has been tracking down Bruno (and Guy), and the book ends on a somewhat melodramatic note with Guy confessing in a Texas hotel room to Miriam's former lover, and to a concealed recording device planted by Gerard.

Strangers on a Train is a remarkably accomplished first novel. Accordingly, we are not surprised to find certain themes, techniques, and ideas to which the author was to return. There are, first of all, two men tied (on one side, unwillingly) to one another, with more than a suggestion that on one side, at least, the bond is erotic. Moreover, the less-than-convincing—at times verging on the clichéd—manner in which the author motivates her characters' behavior, in effect a pseudomotivation, undercuts any recourse to psychological explanation.[4] This ultimately denies the rationality of human behavior, something that is underlined in Bruno's brief *plaidoyer* for the motiveless crime, the *acte gratuit* of existentialist fiction that traces its lineage from Dostoyevsky's *Notes from Underground* (1863) through Gide's *Lafcadio's Adventures* (1914) down to Camus's *Stranger* (1942), a book published in English in 1946, only a few years before Highsmith wrote *Strangers on a Train*.[5]

The authorial hints that Bruno is a latent homosexual are a prime example of the stock quality of the characterization belying its intent. Bruno's deep attachment to his mother, with whom he frequently travels —with whom he in a sense lives—is noted on a number of occasions: "Dully, with a wistful realization that much would happen before he saw them again, he watched his mother's legs flex as she tightened her stockings. The slim lines of her legs always gave him a lift, made him proud. His mother had the best-looking legs he had ever seen on anyone, no matter what age" (*Strangers*, 56). Moreover, Bruno's misogyny is evident in his declaration that there is "essentially one kind of woman! . . . Two-timers. At one end it's two-timing and the other end it's a whore! Take your choice!" (*Strangers*, 25) (he has declared his mother the lone exception to this). Bruno envies and is attracted to Guy because he is a "guy," able to attract "nice" women like Anne and to have a useful "masculine" career, like architecture. Finally, lest we miss the point, when Bruno takes a cruise with his mother, it is on a ship named "The Fairy Prince." This is all a little too pat, even for the 1950s. By opting for such simplistic psychologizing, Highsmith undercuts the efficacy of any psychology. Just as the explanation that Guy's reluctance to tell the police about Bruno derives from an apparent unwillingness to accuse a possibly innocent person of murder, so the attempt to explain Bruno's actions as those of a frustrated homosexual does not convince.

Highsmith thematizes the *acte gratuit* (something radically at variance with such psychologizing) when Bruno delivers his brief for the motiveless crime at his first meeting with Guy on the train. Expatiating on how "everybody ought to do everything it's possible to do before he dies," Bruno tells Guy, "And I did a robbery. . . . Not to get anything. . . . I didn't want what I took. I especially took what I didn't want" (*Strangers*, 19). The reasoning behind Bruno's plan is that it can be done with impunity owing to the killers' apparent lack of motive. Because Bruno murders Miriam after Guy has refused Bruno's suggested plan, Bruno can see the killing as motiveless: "a pure murder, without personal motives!" (*Strangers,* 54). His logic, however, is not completely compelling, as his killing Miriam is not entirely unmotivated. After all, he may possibly benefit from it: he would not have murdered her had he not met Guy and thought there was a possibility, however slight, that Guy would reciprocate.

But one of Highsmith's most impressive achievements—not unrelated to her "pseudomotivation"—has been the creation of an effective kind of "tension" or "suspense" that many readers and critics have responded to and characterized in various ways. Graham Greene saw it as a "tension" deriving from "an undefinable oppression" (Greene, 103). Yet the word that better captures this phenomenon is *irritation*. Tension, of the suspenseful kind that Greene himself created, especially in his "entertainments" of the 1930s, has a pleasant aspect to it, like the closing moments of the first movement of a sonata as it returns to its tonic key. There is no pleasantness of this sort in Highsmith's fiction, where irritation creates annoyance, frustration, and even anger in the reader. A good example of this occurs when Bruno appears, uninvited and unexpected, at Guy's wedding to Anne Faulkner:

> Then Mrs. Faulkner put an arm around his neck and kissed his cheek, and over her shoulder he saw Bruno thrusting himself through the door with the same smile, the same pinlike eyes that had already found him. Bruno came straight towards him and stopped, rocking on his feet.
> "My best—best wishes, Guy. You didn't mind if I looked in, did you? It's a happy occasion!"
> "Get out. Get out of here fast."
> Bruno's smile faded hesitantly. "I just got back from Capri," he said in the same hoarse voice. He wore a new dark royal-blue gabardine suit with lapels broad as an evening suit's lapels. "How've you been, Guy? . . . I just wanted to wish you well." Bruno declared. "There it is."
> "Get out," Guy said. "The door's behind you." But he mustn't say any more, he thought. He would lose control.
> "Call a truce, Guy. I want to meet the bride." (*Strangers,* 175)

The complexities of the reader's emotional response at this point are not easily disentangled. We, too, are caught up in the situation, identifying as we do with Guy. Bruno has appeared on the pretext of wishing Guy and Anne well, yet knowing Guy loathes the sight of him. Guy, on the other hand, is trapped and helpless. He realizes that he cannot make a scene and spoil his and Anne's wedding, something Bruno counts on to succeed in his effrontery. What is so irritating for the Guy-identified reader is Bruno's sovereign disregard of Guy's feelings and his commands under the cover of wishing him well; we, along with Guy, feel frustrated at our powerlessness. Bruno acts as if he has not even heard Guy, denying, almost obliterating, the other person. The creation of this irritation is a singular achievement. It is something Highsmith has in common with Kafka, although Kafka placed this irritation in a social context.

The apparent simplicity of Highsmith's prose, the matter-of-fact irrationality of her characters, the oddities that draw our attention to them without really making them exceptional, and the banal middle-class milieux of many of her novels, all these features, oddly enough, sometimes lend her novels the feel of an Enlightenment roman by Voltaire, Diderot, or perhaps most appropriately Sade. In a classic Sadeian novel such as *The Miseries of Virtue,* for example, the powerful male tortures the women he holds in his power in the guise of educating them. Bruno (whose character possesses a distinct sadistic element), throughout the novel, has always been acting to "help" Guy by getting rid of Miriam, who is an impediment to his divorce and career. On several occasions, he states: "Guy, I'm your friend. I *like* you, Guy." At Guy's wedding, Bruno's casual responses to Guy's intense anger heighten the irritation and frustration we feel at Guy's powerlessness. It is as if Guy does not truly exist independently of Bruno. When Bruno says, "I want to meet the bride, Guy," his tone, expressing *his* desire, has something about it of the feudal lord invoking the droit du seigneur while the groom stands impotently aside, powerless to do anything but accept his fate. In the end, Bruno is always the more powerful; a threat always lurks behind his "helpfulness," and this mixture of helpfulness and threat is peculiarly galling. Highsmith's ability to create situations and feelings like these in a style that resolutely seems to deny any kind of complexity again suggests a comparison with Kafka, whose style was similarly free of surface complexity. Indeed, in the work of both authors, the style helps bring to our consciousness the contrast between surface simplicity and hidden complexity.

Strangers on a Train is set in a 1940s upper-middle-class Manhattan and suburban milieu. As with all of Highsmith's novels published in the 1950s (with the exception of her 1958 novel, *A Game for the Living,* which is set in Mexico), these are white, well-educated Americans. We know from a number of details that Highsmith gives us concerning their lives that they are affluent. Anne's family has a boat docked on

Long Island, and her father at one point asks Guy, "Do any hunting?" to which Guy replies, "a little." Bruno's family appears to have real wealth, although Highsmith is even vaguer than usual with respect to the exact source of that wealth, merely noting that Bruno's father owns a factory.

But the key aspect of the middle-class motif, no matter how much wealth the characters may have, is an "independence" granted them by their membership in the free professions and their inherited money. In none of these novels do any of her protagonists work in a bureaucracy, that omnipresent twentieth-century institution. Guy is a freelance architect, sharing an office with another freelancer, and Anne is a designer, working with a partner. The significance of the freedom their professions allow cannot, in the novel's terms, be underestimated. Although they may have to work, their work never involves them in the bureaucratic tangle so characteristic of modern-day work. This freedom allows Highsmith to successfully dematerialize her characters' motivations, allowing them the luxury of a sometimes irrational choice. The anxiety that ordinary job constraints provokes is clear when at one point, because of the pressures that Bruno puts on him, Guy decides to join a firm rather than to continue working on his own.

> "I think I'll take a job soon, Anne."
> She looked up, astoundedly. "A job? You mean with a firm?"
> It was a phrase to be used about other architects, "a job with a firm."
> He nodded, not looking at her. "I feel like it. Something steady with a good salary." (*Strangers*, 169–70)

On the other hand, Bruno's father is presented negatively, partially, we feel, because of his too close connection to material production (he is in the hardware business) and the messy conflicts it involves him in. Indeed, we learn from Bruno that his father is an upward-striving Hungarian immigrant who exploits his workers, and attempting to justify his hate for his father, Bruno notes that the factory workers are on strike. The message from a broader perspective is that such close contact with material production is damning.

We might, finally, note something about Bruno's name in conjunction with his role and background. His full name, Charles Anthony Bruno, suggests that he is Italian American; his father's eastern European origin suggests that he might be Jewish. In either case, he is not of that northern European stock from which Highsmith invariably draws her sympathetic protagonists. As we shall see, the villains in her novels are most often of Latin or eastern European origin, if we are to take their names as valid indicators, and throughout her career, Highsmith persisted in this tendency to give her negatively portrayed characters quasi-ethnic markers. To the extent that she engages in such stereotyping, one might feel a mild racism at work, and at first glance, this, along with the negative depiction of women and the fixation on the white upper-middle class of a Long Island–Connecticut–Manhattan milieu lends a conservative cast to these early novels. Yet it must be noted that such attitudes and such milieux were not remarkable in the 1950s.

Almost a half century after its original publication, *Strangers on a Train* remains an impressive novel. If anything, it now seems even more impressive, as a novel of its times, especially in its quirkily successful use of existentialist themes. Moreover, Highsmith's creation of a psychic intensity that differed from what any of her contemporaries were doing remains a significant achievement.

The Talented Mr. Ripley (1955)

Highsmith's fourth published novel (now quite possibly her best known) introduces Tom Ripley, a character who through *Ripley Underground* (1970), *Ripley's Game* (1974), *The Boy Who Followed Ripley* (1980), and *Ripley under Water* (1990) was to extend over most of Highsmith's career. In the first of the series, she again used as the novel's fulcrum a relationship between two men with strong and now more openly thematized homoerotic overtones. The milieu, however, has shifted to Europe, and the story unfolds among American expatriates living in Italy. In *The Talented Mr. Ripley,* Highsmith also introduces the theme of an individual transforming himself or herself, of the willed construction of a personality, once again suggesting existentialism's emphasis on individual choice free of any hint of determinism through history or genetics. Although this had been present in *Strangers on a Train* (implicit in Bruno's metaphysics of the *acte gratuit*), it had not been as thoroughly supported by plot and characterization.

Once again, the denial of history, of a material analysis of character, is evident in Highsmith's refusal to grant Ripley a history beyond psycho-analytic clichés. Tom Ripley is provided with only the vaguest of biographical data. This feature—the lack of the protagonist's clear historical and biographical determinants—increased from novel to novel in Highsmith's work of the 1950s. Tom is essentially an orphan, raised by an aunt who continues to partially support him with checks made out in odd amounts.[6]

As the novel begins, Tom Ripley is down on his luck, unemployed and temporarily staying with a friend in a cheap rooming house on Manhattan's Third Avenue. One evening, leaving an East Side bar, Tom is followed by an older man who introduces himself as Herbert Greenleaf. He has recognized Tom as a friend of his son, Richard, who has been living in Italy for two years. Dickie Greenleaf shows no signs of returning to the United States to take up work as a boat designer in his father's small but profitable yacht-building firm, Burke-Greenleaf. Believing that Tom is a closer friend of Dickie's than he actually is, Mr. Greenleaf thinks that Tom might have some influence in persuading Dickie to return home. Mr. Greenleaf stakes Tom to a trip to Italy, where he will try to convince Dickie Greenleaf to come back to the United States.

On arriving at Mongibello, the small coastal town south of Naples where Dickie is living, Tom sets out to become Dickie's friend. (In fact, their relationship had been so slight that Dickie does not at first recognize Tom.) Tom also comes to know Dickie's friend Marge Sherwood, who lives in the town. Within a short time, Tom has made friends with Dickie but has had no luck at all in convincing him to return home. Moreover, he soon confesses that this is actually why he has come to Italy and that Dickie's father has paid for the trip. He has, however, sufficiently ingratiated himself with Dickie for Dickie to suggest that Tom move into the house he rents. The two become something like good friends and take a trip to Naples together, extending it to Rome. The relationship continues, pleasantly enough, until one day Dickie discovers Tom in his room trying on his clothes and accessories. This produces a decided tension between them, and although there is no break as such, things are never again the same. Indeed, at this point, they discuss the issue of Tom's sexuality, and Tom denies that he is homosexual.

Tom and Dickie take another trip, and at San Remo, on the Ligurian Coast, they rent a motorboat. Precipitated by a premonition that Dickie is losing interest in him and by Dickie's innuendos that Tom is homosexual, Tom brutally murders Dickie, battering him to death with an oar. Moreover, the description of the murder suggests that it provides a sexual release for Tom, sublimating his desire for Dickie into violence. After the murder, Tom sinks the body and then, with Dickie's money, travels back south. At first he tells Dickie's people that Dickie has decided to stay in Rome for the winter and forges letters to this effect from Dickie to his friends. At one point, Tom rents an apartment in Rome as Richard Greenleaf and is tracked down by a friend of Dickie's, Freddie Miles, whom Tom had met earlier. Because Miles becomes suspicious, Tom kills him, too, and then assumes Dickie's identity completely, altering or fabricating documents to support the switch and picking up Dickie's monthly checks. Eventually, after Dickie's body is found, Tom forges Dickie's will, bequeathing Dickie Greenleaf's money to Tom Ripley, and at the novel's end has succeeded to Dickie's money and possessions while reverting to Tom Ripley.

As noted, one of the most striking characteristics of Highsmith's novels is how little the reader learns of her characters' backgrounds.[7] Although we learn that Tom has been orphaned at an early age and raised by a maiden aunt, we know little of the circumstances of his growing up, nothing of his education, and little about his work experiences. There are large gaps in where he has lived and what he has done. Much that goes to form a personality is omitted in a Highsmith novel, specifically the protagonists' relationship to their parents. They are, in one sense, anti-bildungsromans. Hence, when the novel begins (and we learn nothing subsequently), we know only that Tom is 25 and living a hand-to-mouth existence, a fringe member of a group of middle-class Manhattanites. Somehow, though he has not graduated high school, he has managed to be accepted by them as one of their own. There is a suggestion at the beginning of the novel and in flashbacklike hints later that some members of this crowd are homosexual. It is never more than a suggestion, yet lacking anything else, one at least casually suspects that the bond was originally sexual. But Tom's sexuality is as vague as is his class and work history. The effect of all these omissions is that Tom Ripley is still—at 25—essentially undefined. A further result is that he becomes defined, but not formed, through his actions in the course of the novel. On the overt social level, the primary effect is to bracket out any reference to history or biography, an effect that setting the novel among expatriates in Europe heightens. The existentialist precept that one is constantly defining oneself through the choices one makes—that one is free to do so, indeed, must do so—is here facilitated through Highsmith's refusal to provide Ripley with a history, personal or social, that might define him. Ripley constructs himself in the novel, sometimes quite literally, as when he gains weight to look more like Dickie Greenleaf. "Whatever our being may be," Sartre asserted in *Being and Nothingness,* it is a choice" (Sartre, 607). This is surely true of Tom Ripley.

Because the reader knows nothing in the way of traditional historical and biographical particulars, the question of the motivation of Ripley's behavior is thrown into the present. With a significant exception, no aspect of Ripley's character is seen to derive in any material way from his past—his upbringing and education—something that holds generally for Highsmith's protagonists. As noted, Tom has not completed high school. Three months on a banana boat and a similar length of time as a stockroom clerk with the IRS constitute our knowledge of his jobs, experience that seems singularly ill-matched to his attitudes and qualities, so disparate, indeed, as only to emphasize the lack of congruence between lived experience and character.[8] When Tom sees Dickie's paintings, he thinks: "It wasn't good in his opinion, probably in anybody's opinion. . . . [The landscapes] were all wild and hasty and monotonously similar. The combination of terra cotta and electric blue was in nearly every one, terra cotta roofs and mountains and bright electric blue seas. It was the blue he had puts in Marge's eyes, too."[9] Even before meeting Dickie, Tom picks out a bathrobe for him (as a gift from Dickie's parents) that is inferior in Tom's own eyes but that he thinks Dickie will like. (Dickie does.)

The most important event in the novel, Tom's murder of Dickie, is important not only for reasons of plot but also for its revelation of the novel's amoral worldview, one implicit in much of Highsmith's fiction. Here, as in other novels, the reader has been skillfully led to sympathize with Tom, a murderer. One appropriate point for discussing the subtheme of Tom's sexuality as the immediate impetus for the murder is that his friendly and quasi-sexual overtures to Dickie have been contemptuously rebuffed. (The second, and no less important, is that Tom wants the gracious lifestyle Dickie's money will provide.)

Before the murder, Dickie had begun to tire of Tom, even making a casual inquiry as to when Tom was returning to the States. They had planned to take a trip together to Paris, but Dickie has now reduced that to San Remo. The handwriting is on the wall: "Dickie was in a slightly more cheerful mood, but the awful finality was still there, the feeling that this was the last trip that they would make together anywhere" (*Ripley,* 84). As a sop to Tom, Dickie agrees to go to Cannes. "At least Cannes is France" (*Ripley,* 85), Tom notes reproachfully.

But Dickie's behavior on the trip makes it clear that he no longer regards Tom as a friend. While strolling around Cannes with Dickie, Tom admires a group of acrobats practicing on the beach, and Dickie sardonically suggests Tom's interest is sexual. Dickie continues to

behave in an unfriendly manner on the trip back to San Remo (even letting Tom pick up the tab for the hotel). On the train back to Italy, "Tom
stared at Dickie's closed eyelids. A crazy emotion of hate, of affection, of
impatience and frustration was swelling in him, hampering his breathing. He wanted to kill Dickie. It was not the first time he had thought
of it" (*Ripley,* 87). Hence, the motive for killing Dickie comes from
Dickie's contempt for him and from what Tom sees as Dickie's rejection
of his friendship. In something like a replay of *Strangers on a Train,* Tom
has inherited Bruno's role, and this is evident in his feeling rejected by
Dickie (as Bruno had felt rejected by Guy). Here, however, the reader's
sympathies have switched to the disturbed individual, and the fact that
Dickie is a much less admirable figure than Guy Haines underlines the
shift in Highsmith's sympathies.

The sexual nature of Tom's feelings is clear in the violent scene in
which he bludgeons Dickie to death with the oar: "[H]e could have hit
Dickie, sprung on him, or kissed him, or thrown him overboard" (*Ripley,*
90). Immediately before assaulting Dickie, "He picked up the oar, as
casually as if he were playing with it between his knees, and when
Dickie was shoving his trousers down [he is wearing trousers over his
swimming trunks and is preparing to swim], Tom lifted the oar" (*Ripley,*
90–91). Although Highsmith is suggesting that Ripley's violence
results from his feelings of rejection and acts as a kind of substitute for
sex, any explication of Highsmith's use of the homoerotic theme needs
further analysis. Its function, as well as the function of sexuality in general in the novel, is carefully controlled and serves a number of purposes.

Most striking is that Tom Ripley is not, in point of fact, a homosexual. There is never any indication in the novel that he has had sex with a
man (or a woman, for that matter), though there are a number of indications that he is interested in men. At the beginning of the novel, there
is a hint that one of the bars he frequents is a gay bar, and this is recalled
later when Tom is trying to decide if Dickie is homosexual. In New
York, Tom is sharing a room with a man who does department store
windows, which in 1950s Manhattan would suggest that the man is a
homosexual. When Mr. Greenleaf is showing Tom a photo album,
preparatory to his trip to Europe, Tom thinks: "The album was not
interesting to him until Richard got to be sixteen or so, long-legged,
slim, with the wave tightening in his hair" (*Ripley,* 19). In Europe there
are further hints: a young boy in whom Tom has shown interest and,
most explicitly, Marge's comments on his character to Dickie.

But Tom never comes close to making a sexual advance to Dickie. The best time they ever have is the night they spend wandering around Rome when they take a girl home. In fact, the moment is particularly revealing. Asexually, they "protect" the girl, the two of them chaperoning her home in a cab without making the least sexual advance to her. Tom's comment on the event is significant: "Typical Americans would have raped her." (Tom's most rewarding relationship with a woman was with Cleo, a friend in New York, a relationship in which, by mutual agreement, they ruled out sex.) In Italy, the discussion that Tom and Dickie have concerning Tom's sexuality ends with Dickie's taunt "that Marge thinks you don't even *have* any sexual interest," something that Tom indirectly confirms in his own thoughts. With respect to Tom's behavior in the novel, this characterization would seem to be the most appropriate. But this is also true of Dickie Greenleaf, whom Tom at first suspects (incorrectly) of having an affair with Marge, who wants such a relationship with Dickie. (In general, in Highsmith's novels, women are more interested in sex than are men.) What is striking in all this is the total absence of sexuality from the novel. Even among minor or peripheral characters, no sexual relationship is shown; in fact, it is hard to think of the appearance of couples. The only marriage depicted is that of Dickie's parents, and his mother is sick and may die at any moment.

Yet because the plethora of hints never blossoms into full-fledged homosexuality, the question as to its function arises. Why are we given hint upon hint, only in the end to have nothing materialize? I think Tom's failing to act on his own sexual impulses has to be seen in connection with Dickie's refusal to have a romance with Marge and with the absence of any rewarding relationships, whether homosexual or heterosexual, in the novel. This absence underscores the extreme isolation of these individuals. Moreover, as one critic has suggested, it is Tom Ripley's very indeterminacy, including his sexual indeterminacy, that attracts the reader to him: "To anchor Tom's identity in latent homosexuality . . . is to read against the clear indications in Highsmith's novel that Tom's strength is in his indeterminacy of identity, in an emptiness of self that allows the superior performance of roles."[10] Yet Tom's emptiness, his lack of relatedness to others, has further effects. It contributes to the aura of isolation that envelops the characters, primarily Ripley, but to a lesser extent Dickie and Marge as well. Tom views such isolation positively. Alone in Rome, "Every moment to Tom was a pleasure, alone in his room or walking the streets of Rome. . . . It was impossible ever to be lonely or bored" (*Ripley,* 106). Later he goes to a nightclub and orders "a superb dinner which he ate in elegant solitude at a candlelit table for two. He did not at all mind dining and going to the theatre alone" (*Ripley,* 116). Even in moments when Tom is with Dickie in Rome, the forced quality of their "togetherness" creates a sense of claustrophobia that the novel's hermetic expatriate milieu does nothing to lessen.

What, then, constitutes Tom Ripley's pleasures? Here, I think, we come to a subtext of the novel that does not seem to have been consciously inserted into the novel (as have the suggestions of Ripley's homosexuality) and that will become increasingly prominent in Highsmith's novels, to such an extent, indeed, that it can be said to constitute something of their true content. What constitutes this latent level of the novel is its fascination with objects, or what might be termed the novel's parti pris for commodities, the objects that consumer society produces to be bought and possessed, which through such purchase and possession serve to define their owner. "With *all* possession," Sartre wrote in the phenomenological analyses entitled "Doing and Having," "there is made the crystallizing synthesis which Stendhal has described for the one case of love. Each possessed object which raises itself on the foundation of the world manifests the entire world. . . . To appropriate this object is then to appropriate the world symbolically" (Sartre, 760). A good example of this appears in an otherwise inconsequential description of Ripley's passage on a train back to southern Italy after he has murdered Dickie:

> The white taut sheets of his berth on the train seemed the most wonderful luxury he had ever known. He caressed them with his hand before he turned the light out. And the clean blue-grey blankets, the spanking efficiency of the little black net over his head—Tom had an ecstatic moment when he thought of all the pleasures that lay before him now with Dickie's money, other beds, tables, seas, ships, suitcases, shirts, years of freedom, years of pleasure. Then he turned the light out and put his head down and almost at once fell asleep, happy, content, and utterly confident, as he had never been before in his life. (*Ripley,* 97)

This is the most revealing moment in the novel, not only for what it says about Tom Ripley but for the dynamic it lends the novel. Tom's joy at the "taut" sheets and the "spanking" efficiency of the little black net over his head provides a way into Ripley's character. The efficient net, especially, epitomizes all that Tom (and many of Highsmith's protagonists) understand by pleasure, and the language of the passage effectively presents the real pleasure that Tom receives from such objects. This passage is charged—almost sexually—with a passion unlike anything else in the novel. For the only time in the novel, we see Tom truly fulfilled. (We will see similar scenes in the novels discussed in the next chapter.) It is striking that in the list of prospective pleasures that Tom sees Dickie's money enabling him to enjoy, none has to do with people. The only item even vaguely suggestive of organic sensuality is "seas," and it seems oddly out of place. Tom has cathected his libido onto things, and with a vengeance. Marge's suggestion that Tom is asexual is corroborated here. Snug in his compartment (which is far too clean and aseptic to suggest a womb), embraced by the sterility of the white sheets, the blue-gray blankets, and the black net, Tom has found his perfect habitat, in which there is literally no room for another person. There is a direct equation as well as a very powerful emotional connection between things and pleasure and freedom; Tom is not one who feels that material possessions weigh one down. Moreover, the absence of people is striking. Even more than in most of Highsmith's novels, we have in *The Talented Mr. Ripley* a character who creates himself through, and is defined by, objects.

In one sense, Tom is a forerunner of the replicants in the 1981 film *Blade Runner*. The replicants mimic humans to perfection (indeed, in human terms, they go beyond perfection, much as Tom sees himself as a more perfect Dickie Greenleaf than the real Dickie could ever be) but, lacking memory, are forced to take their cues from real-life models; as Tom lacks a history, he too can be seen as lacking memory. Tom's real-life model is Dickie, whom Tom physically models himself after, gaining a little weight and lightening his hair to complete the imitation. He tries on Dickie's rings, monogrammed shirts, and cuff links—"my God," Dickie says when he discovers Tom in his room, "even the shoes"—and when learning Italian is careful not to become too colloquial, avoiding a frequent use of the subjunctive because Dickie did not use it often. Indeed, at one point in the novel, he succeeds so well that, forced for a moment to revert to Tom Ripley, he has to consciously produce *that* role.

Because things, rather than people, provide the objects for Tom's emotions and desires, he has an aesthetics, rather than an ethics.[11] Hence it is no accident that he becomes involved in art forgeries in the later novels. Things take precedence over people, and emotions revolve around things. Nowhere in the novel does Tom reveal for individuals the passion he has shown for things, not even for Dickie, who, as critics have pointed out, is not a particularly admirable individual.[12] Whereas this fascination with objects became even more pronounced in Highsmith's next novels, these two important novels from Highsmith's first decade as a novelist establish themes that remain significant for some time to come: the problematics of human relationships and the fascination of commodities. As we shall see, these themes are not unrelated. Moreover, the power of fantasy suggested in aspects of Bruno and Ripley will increase in prominence. In three novels that Highsmith published between 1957 and 1962, these themes will be enacted within the confines (and that is the appropriate word) of an established or desired domesticity. Odd though it might at first seem for a writer whose protagonists often seem to be living in emotional isolation booths, their confrontation with the demands of domestic life produced a series of novels (in my estimation Highsmith's finest) whose odd but intense power rival any created by her contemporaries.

A Note on the Subsequent Ripley Novels

What ties all later Ripley novels together is the theme of domesticity. The central figures through which that theme is represented are Ripley, his wife Heloise (often more an absence than a presence), his domestic servant Madame Annette, and, most important of all, Belle Ombre, the gated house where Ripley lives his domestic idyll. The marriage is, naturally, childless. More than the mafiosi who occasionally threaten Ripley's life, more than Murchison, the Texas art connoisseur who suspects the forged Derwatts, more, finally, than the American couple who in *Ripley under Water* take up residence in the same town and most threaten the idyll, more than all of these, a child would unbalance the blissful but fragile ecology that is Ripley's Belle Ombre existence. No matter how threatening the outside world might become, there is always this refuge, and Ripley is most mobilized when this home is threatened. One cannot imagine Tom Ripley in any frenetic urban milieu—London or Paris— where the sheer number of chance passersby would present an unacceptable level of threat. Here, in small-town, exurban France, the odd car passing along the road in front of his house is enough to alert Ripley to a state of readiness. To introduce a child into this milieu would be to introduce at the same time the random, uncontrollable disorder of everyday life. Although one should not underestimate the opportunity for heightened tasteful consumption on the part of the Ripleys (one can imagine the various items of apparel, children's games, music lessons, ski lessons, choice private schools, and tutors that the possession of a child would call forth) that such an addition to their menage would allow, in the end the child would too much disturb that perfectly balanced triad of Tom, Heloise, and Madame Annette, a union that no other in all of Highsmith's novels comes close to matching in its tranquillity and calm pleasures.

Indeed, the last four novels in the series function within Highsmith's oeuvre as a kind of refuge from the bitter, tormented relationships that otherwise characterize the world of her novels. Moreover, part of the reason that the Ripley novels lack the emotional (if not the plot) tension so otherwise all-pervasive in her fiction is the lack of conflict between Ripley and Heloise, between whom disagreements never rise above the level of a conflict over when they should begin their next vacation. In a sense, these novels functioned as a kind of breather for Highsmith, a fictional place to which she could repair from time to time when the otherwise quite gruesome business of social interaction in her more ambitious novels became too much. This becomes clear from the series of tortured novels she published between 1957 and 1962, discussed in the next chapter. In these novels, it is suggested that the *No Exit* quality of social life can end only in death.

Highsmith has remarked that Ripley does not seem very interested in sex, and here is one instance in which we would accord her correct. Sex, in these novels, would seem to be for Ripley somewhat analogous to one of the finer wines in his cave: something to be appreciated on a special occasion, definitely not a part of everyday life. This view provokes no objections from Heloise. One might also speculate that having sex more often would increase the chances of Heloise's becoming pregnant, something to be avoided.

Chapter Three
Hell Is Other People

The other side of the fantasy represented by Tom Ripley's life of domestic bliss at Belle Ombre is revealed in a series of novels portraying domestic life as one of the most harrowing human experiences. *Deep Water* (1957), *This Sweet Sickness* (1960), and *The Cry of the Owl* (1962) represent a change in Highsmith's interests. Were it not for the reputation she had achieved as a suspense novelist (aided in large part by the success of Hitchcock's film version of *Strangers on a Train*), she might well have achieved, as a result of these novels, a reputation as a serious novelist much earlier than she did. Although her 1952 novel *The Blunderer* was a first step in her exploration of American domesticity and the role of the community, she best realized that representation in the three novels published between 1957 and 1962. Moreover, her interest in this aspect of life reflects a concern of American literature at this moment in U.S. social history. The middle-class migration from the cities to the suburbs was in full swing, and although Highsmith does not represent this movement directly, these novels do, idiosyncratically and obliquely, reflect this demographic *volte-face*. Moreover, in all three novels, Highsmith focuses on a severely circumscribed community (in which "public opinion" plays an important role), to such a degree that this community becomes, in a sense, the world, *tout court*. Hence, there results a political dimension to these works.

Furthermore, it is not just the suburbs but the society's fixation with that arch-symbol of the American dream, the freestanding house, that in two of these novels holds the protagonists in its thrall. In this, again, Highsmith was not alone. Two of the most successful novels of the early 1960s, Richard Yates's *Revolutionary Road* (1961) and Bruce Jay Friedman's *Stern* (1962), present the suburban house as a quasi protagonist. But those novels use more traditional modes of social criticism, whereas Highsmith's refract the object through a lens that distorts but through that very distortion reveals a truth not apparent in the more conventional perspective of her peers.

Last, as a faint and perverse phosphorescent afterimage of the McCarthy-era witch-hunts, a subtle political subtext leaves its troubling glow on the little civil societies of these novels, especially *The Cry of the Owl*. In all three novels, an accused or suspect individual comes into conflict with the community. What gives this theme its oddly perverse twist is that although the community is always proved to be wrong, in *Deep Water* and in *This Sweet Sickness,* it supports a murderer, and in *The Cry of the Owl,* it condemns and convicts an innocent man.

Deep Water (1957)

Deep Water is one of Highsmith's most accomplished novels, and Anthony Boucher accurately characterized it as a "full-fleshed novel of pity and irony."[1] In it Highsmith attempts a thorough analysis of her protagonist's motivation (though again the analysis fails to convince). More remarkable is that for the first time (setting aside, for the moment, *The Price of Salt*), Highsmith portrays an independent female character. Furthermore, in distinct contrast to *Strangers on a Train* and *The Talented Mr. Ripley*, the setting is tightly localized in exurban, small-town, familial America. Last, the events unfold within a marriage, and the most striking difference vis-à-vis the earlier novels is that the Van Allens not only are married but also have a child, forming a constellation whose typicality was not to be matched until *People Who Knock on the Door,* more than a quarter century later (at a time when such a constellation was no longer typical).

Deep Water focuses on the relationship between Victor Van Allen and his wife, Melinda. Vic, Melinda, and their daughter Trixie (Beatrice) live in Little Wesley, a Berkshire town where Vic owns and runs (with an assistant) Greenspur Press, a small, quality publishing house, financed by Vic's considerable trust-fund income ($40,000 a year in the mid-1950s). The Van Allens, especially Vic, are respected members of the community. The problem (though it is not necessarily seen as a problem by Vic) is the blatant flirtatiousness, and sometime infidelity, of Melinda, who has apparently been unfaithful to Vic before the novel opens and has several affairs in its course. Perhaps more accurately, the problem is Vic's apparent refusal to react to these affairs, followed by his subsequent overdetermined responses. Together, they determine the course of the novel.

Melinda Van Allen has been "headstrong and spoilt" almost from the beginning; indeed, this had been one of her attractions for Vic.[2] But after she gives birth to Trixie, she becomes disenthralled with their marriage: "Vic supposed that the conventionality of having a baby, plus being a wife was more than her constitutional rebelliousness could bear"

(*Deep,* 22). She begins having affairs.[3] As the novel begins, Vic has "confessed" to Joel Nash that he has murdered Malcolm McCrae, Melinda's former lover, because Vic suspects that Joel is currently having an affair with Melinda. (McCrae has been found murdered in New York, but Vic was not in fact involved in his death.) Vic makes his "confession" at a party and scares off Nash, who ceases his involvement with Melinda. But Vic's "confession" also makes its way through the community of Little Wesley. Although most people do not believe the story, they nevertheless view Vic's lie as being in bad taste. (Eventually the real killer confesses, and Vic is completely absolved of the crime by the community.) But although Joel has been scared off, it is clear that this has not resolved the issue of Melinda's behavior.

After Vic has been cleared of McCrae's murder, Melinda becomes friends with Charles De Lisle, recently arrived in Little Wesley for a six-week engagement playing the piano at a local bar. Melinda begins to see De Lisle often and even starts taking piano lessons from him. The description of Melinda's intensifying relationship with De Lisle is worth quoting at length because it gives the flavor of how her relationships are depicted by the narrator, perceived by Vic, and defended by Melinda:

> Vic knew what was happening, and he tried to make Melinda admit it and stop it before it got all over town. He simply told her, in a quiet way, that he thought she was seeing too much of Charley De Lisle.
> "You're imagining things," she said. "The first person I've been able to talk to in weeks without being treated like a pariah, and you hate it. You don't want me to get any fun out of life, that's all!"
> She could say things like that to him as if she really meant them. She could actually stymie him and make him wonder if she really believed what she said. In an effort to be fair with her, he tried to see it the way she told it, tried to imagine that it was impossible that she could be attracted to a greasy, sick-looking night-club entertainer. But he couldn't see it that way. She had made the same denials in regard to Jo-Jo, and Jo-Jo had been equally repellent from Vic's point of view, and yet *that* had happened. Jo-Jo had been so amusing, a laugh a minute. He'd been so nice to Trixie. Now Charley De Lisle was such a wonderful piano player. He was showing her how to improve her playing. He came over a couple of afternoons a week now, after three when Vic had left the house, and he gave Melinda a lesson until five when he had to go to work at the Lord Chesterfield. Trixie was generally home in the afternoons, so what was the harm in his coming over? But sometimes Melinda wasn't home for lunch, and sometimes they didn't play the piano in the afternoon,

because an ash-tray that Vic had seen on the keyboard at two o'clock would be there when he got home at seven. Sometimes they were up at Charley De Lisle's house, where there wasn't a piano.

"Just what do you expect me to think about this?" Vic asked her.

"Nothing! I don't know what you're up in the air about!" (*Deep*, 69–70)

What most upsets Vic is the prospect of having his reputation suffer if it becomes known that his wife is having another affair. While having a drink with a friend, Horace Mellers, Vic thinks: "The Mellers haven't seen Melinda and Charlie together yet. It'd take them only two minutes, if they ever saw them together, to know what was happening" (*Deep*, 76).

Shortly thereafter, De Lisle is engaged as a pianist for a costume party where he is introduced by Melinda, who spends much of the party with him: "Melinda and De Lisle were simply sitting on the piano bench talking to each other. But Melinda's face had that warm animation that Vic for many years had not seen directed towards himself" (*Deep*, 86). Vic thinks it will soon be obvious that the two are romantically involved. As the evening progresses, various guests go for a swim in the hosts' pool. At one point, only Vic and Charley are in the pool, and Vic realizes that no one is on the terrace.

> De Lisle was on his back, floating. One of his white arms came up and lashed the water awkwardly and a little frantically, though where he was would be barely over his head, Vic knew. Vic would have loved to grab him by the shoulders and hold him under, and even as he thought of it, Vic swam towards him. De Lisle was now making an overhead stroke to bring him to the edge of the pool, but Vic reached him in a second, grabbed his throat and pulled him backward. There was not even a bubble as De Lisle's head went under. Vic had him under the chin and by one shoulder now, and unconsciously he tugged him towards where the water was over Vic's head, though it was easy to keep his own head above the surface because of De Lisle's threshing efforts to rise under his hands. Vic made a scissor-like movement with his legs and caught both of De Lisle's thighs between his calves. Vic's head went under as he tipped backwards, but his hands kept their grip and he pulled himself forward and rose again. De Lisle was still under.
>
> It's a joke, Vic thought to himself. If he were to let him up now, it would be merely a joke, though perhaps a rough one, but just then De Lisle's efforts grew violent, and Vic concentrated his own effort, one hand on the back of De Lisle's neck now, his other hand holding De Lisle's wrist away from him under the water. De Lisle's free hand was ineffectual

against Vic's grip on the back of his neck. One of De Lisle's feet broke
the surface of the water, then disappeared. (*Deep*, 90–91)

Vic has murdered De Lisle.

One thing to note is the specific motivation for the act. The shift
from the conditional ("would have loved . . .") to the indicative is a little
odd. It is as if the narrator has elided the actual moment of decision,
suggesting that there had not really been a decision. And it is not until
the second paragraph, after Vic toys with the idea of releasing De Lisle,
that Vic seems to have decided. Even this is subtly shifted away from Vic
by the suggestion that he is acting in response to De Lisle's intensifying
struggle, almost as if De Lisle precipitates his own murder. This de-
emphasizing of conscious choice reverses the emphasis on the freely
choosing individual that played so prominent a role in *Strangers on a
Train* and *The Talented Mr. Ripley*. Taken in conjunction with the increasing role of the community, this reversal suggests a shift in Highsmith's
worldview. Indeed, in *Deep Water*, it is Melinda who is the existentialist of
choice.

After De Lisle's body has been found, Melissa accuses Vic of having
killed him: " '*You* did it,' Melinda said, looking at Vic. 'I bet you hit him
on the head and held him under' " (*Deep*, 97). She repeats the accusation
at the coroner's inquest: "*Yes*, I think my husband had something to do
with it! I think he *did* it!" (*Deep*, 107). Afterward, she tells her friends
that she thinks Vic murdered De Lisle, even going so far as to hire a
detective to investigate and observe Vic. But Vic realizes what the man
is and, as he is paying the bills (he becomes suspicious when he discovers
Melinda making large withdrawals from his bank account), calls up the
detective agency and cancels the arrangement, with typical aplomb
identifying himself as the object of surveillance.

Shortly thereafter, Melinda forms a friendship with Tony Cameron, a
contractor. This develops into the most serious of her liaisons, and she
eventually accepts Vic's offer of a divorce (something she had earlier
refused) and makes plans to fly to Mexico with Cameron. Vic again inter-
venes and murders Cameron, and again the act is not premeditated. Driving through town, Vic sees Cameron outside what he assumes is the law
office where Melinda is filing the divorce papers: "Vic saw him when he
was about half a block in front of him on the right side of the street, and
not really knowing what he was about . . ." (*Deep*, 207). On the pretext
of showing Cameron a type of marble he may be able to use in his work,
Vic takes him to an abandoned quarry, where Vic throws two large rocks

at him, knocking him off the ledge and down into the quarry. Cameron dies in the fall, and Vic sinks the body in the water of the quarry.

At first Vic avoids arrest because Cameron's body is never found. But in the end, Melinda and Don Wilson (a friend, but not a lover) lure Vic into revealing that the body is in the quarry, thereby incriminating himself. When, in the last pages of the novel, he realizes he has been discovered (and seconds before the police arrive to arrest him), he brutally murders Melinda.

Deep Water is in my opinion Highsmith's finest novel. It mutes and transmutes a number of the themes that were salient in *Strangers on a Train* and *The Talented Mr. Ripley* while its conventional setting heightens the contrast of extreme irrationality with everyday life and allows Highsmith to explore the issues of domesticity and community. Highsmith's plots are often effective, but we should not overlook the extent to which they are a function of her characters, as in this novel of Vic Van Allen's unconventional relationship with his wife and the psyche it bespeaks.[4]

Deep Water is a study of domestic psychic violence, and the first question readers ask with respect to the Van Allens' marriage is why Vic does not initially react more forcefully to Melinda's flirtatiousness and possible infidelities. The answer is complex. Sexual relations between Vic and Melinda have ceased some time before the novel begins, and Vic is depicted as uninterested in Melinda sexually (although this is occasionally contradicted at key moments). But he is upset at her behavior and even at times jealous of her. Yet, if we are to believe Vic, what upsets him stems not so much from Melinda's unfaithfulness as from her brazen manner as well as what Vic sees as her poor choice of lovers: "It was not that he objected to Melinda's having affairs with other men, per se . . . it was that she picked such idiotic, spineless characters and that she let it leak out all over town" (*Deep,* 21). Commenting on two of her lovers, he says, "I found them both terrible bores and terribly beneath you" (*Deep,* 40) and "He wouldn't object to her having a man of some stature and self-respect, a man with some ideas in his head, as a lover, Vic thought. But he was afraid Melinda would never choose that kind or that that kind would never choose her. Vic could visualize a kind of charitable, fair-minded, civilized arrangement in which all three of them might be happy and benefit from contact with one another" (*Deep,* 41), a vision underlined by a reference to Goethe's novel *Elective Affinities.*

But Vic's behavior works against the reader's seriously considering Vic's assertion that he could tolerate such a sophisticated arrangement.

It seems more Vic's toying with a concept than a realistic suggestion on his part, and his homicidal violence suggests he is kidding himself about his capacity to tolerate sharing Melinda. On the other hand, a reading of Vic as someone out of touch with his feelings, while somewhat more plausible, is also unsatisfying because of the chasm between Vic's urbane superficial amiability and his murderous impulses; "out of touch" does not suggest the unbridgeable gulf that lies between Vic's behavior and his ratiocination. As Thomas Sutcliffe noted, "[Highsmith's] suburban killers remain calculatingly evasive until the end (death follows death for the sake of concealment rather than gratification). They don't hear voices and they don't have fun."[5] Although the novel may also be read as the description of a progressive schizophrenic breakdown, Vic does not seem disturbed or lose touch with reality until quite near the end of the novel. Here, we are at its beginning. As conventional motivation, Highsmith's attempts to lend a psychological underpinning to Vic fail. Closer to the truth is her ability "to write not about what it feels like to be mad, but what it feels like to remain sane while committing the actions of a madman" (Sutcliffe, 1118).

Highsmith does, however, go to great lengths to tell us things about Vic that in another author would be seen as "bringing a character to life." Vic knows Latin and is interested in insects, crustacea, and modern poetry. He has his preferences in music—Bach and Gregorian chants. He has equally strong dislikes, too. In fact, Vic is all preferences and aversions. Hardly a page goes by without Vic expressing a strong like or dislike or discriminating something as being in good or bad taste. But all such markers bring us no closer to understanding why Vic does or does not act as he does toward Melinda and her lovers. We are left in Klein's "vacant lot." Such qualities become almost things, like purchases, remaining apart from Vic rather than a part of him. Every attempt of the narrator or of Vic himself to explain or justify his behavior remains unconvincing. For example, early in the novel, the narrator notes: "One of Vic's firmest principles was that everybody—therefore a wife—should be allowed to do as she pleased, provided no one else was hurt" (*Deep*, 21). People cannot really be characterized through their formulation of principles, and this is really a begging of the question.

Highsmith attempts neither representative typicality nor individual authenticity but rather something quite different, something like an ideal-type, the agglomeration of whose traits are found nowhere "in nature," although individually such traits are unexceptional.[6] Again, such characters resemble the protagonists of Enlightenment *contes*. They are neither real nor false. Rather, they represent an idea of a certain character rather than a character itself. Nor are they "flat" as opposed to "rounded" characters, to borrow the well-known categories established by E. M. Forster in *Aspects of the Novel* (1927). Perhaps Highsmith's characters are best suggested by saying that they constitute bundles of attitudes. In one sense, this accounts for the hyper-cerebral nature of such psyches and their cerebralized emotions. Such characterization, although not conventionally realist, can be effective. Its abstract quality lends it power, just as the masks used in Japanese No drama, which, though incapable of the subtlety of expression of the human face, by that very reduction and abstraction produce a powerful effect unattainable by the more plastic human countenance.

A second question (also crucial to the plot) about the Van Allens' marriage concerns Melinda Van Allen: Why does she continue living with someone she believes to have murdered, not once, but twice? Melinda, too, acts irrationally. In any rational world, it would be hard to imagine someone continuing to live with a person she firmly believes is a murderer. Moreover, her situation is not a case of abused-woman syndrome or an exploration of a masochistic psychological dependence: Melinda is neither masochistic nor abused. Just as in *Strangers on a Train* there was no rational reason for Guy Haines not to notify the police of his suspicions about Bruno having murdered Miriam, so in *Deep Water* Melinda's behavior in staying with Vic is irrational, "absurd," and—her choice.

The novel's attempt to analyze Melinda's flirtatious behavior also lacks plausibility. When Vic talks the situation over with a psychiatrist, "The only new idea the psychiatrist put into his head was that Melinda, like many women who have a child might be 'finished' with him as a man and as a husband, now that he had given her the child. . . . Vic's explanation was that plain contrariness had motivated her in rejecting him: she knew he still loved her, so she chose to give him no satisfaction by showing that she loved him in return" (*Deep,* 23). Ultimately, Highsmith's explanation of Melinda is no explanation at all. Attributing Melinda's behavior to a contrarian nature relies on an analysis that effectively asserts an arbitrary dynamic to human behavior. Although the psychiatrist's suggestion could under other circumstances be explored, nothing in the way that Highsmith presents Melinda leads us to take such an opinion seriously. Rather, it reconfirms an impression of the author's lack of interest in such conventional motivation. Indeed, Vic's interpretation of Melinda's contrariness underlines such lack of interest because such an explanation explains nothing, denying anything like the complexity that determines human personality and behavior by reducing everything to a quirk.

But if Vic's or Melinda's motivation cannot be illuminated by traditional characterization, there are other moments and constellations that approach what I suggest is one of the novel's authentic dynamics. One such moment occurs at the end of the novel, when the uproar over Cameron's disappearance has abated and Vic is breathing easier. Melinda has begun to act quite friendly toward him, even to the point of hinting at reestablishing sexual relations between them. Vic, though he mistrusts Melinda's motives, cannot help feeling more kindly toward her. Melinda, Trixie, and a few friends have arranged a surprise birthday party for Vic: "Then came the presents. Melinda handed him three tied-together boxes from Brooks Brothers, each of which contained a sweater—one a mustard-colored coat sweater, one blue and red, which was an Italian import, and the third a white tennis sweater with a red stripe. Vic adored good sweaters. He was touched to the point of feeling a lump in his throat that Melinda had given him three" (*Deep*, 241–42). There is a final, special gift, also from Melinda:

> It was a Geiger counter complete with headphone, probe, and shoulder strap. There were even ore samples. Vic was speechless, delighted. He went to Melinda and put his arm around her.
> "Melinda—thanks," he said, and pressed his lips against her cheek.
> (*Deep*, 242)

This emphasis on consumer goods—food, clothes, books, records—has been apparent throughout the novel. They do far more than provide atmosphere; they do more than characterize Vic and others (their ostensible purpose). Both the frequency of such "characterizations" and the emotionally charged language of the individual passages in which they appear suggest that at times objects themselves are the subject of the text, that is, the agent determining the action. More than any of Highsmith's previous characters, Vic seems defined by his relationship to things. The lump in his throat at the gift of the three sweaters and the affectionate kiss for the Geiger counter are in fact among the most moving moments for Vic in the novel, akin, but deeper, in the emotional charge of Vic's reaction, to Tom Ripley's "ecstasy" in his sleeping compartment on the train from San Remo to Rome.

Such reactions are all the more striking because unlike Bruno, Guy, or Tom, Vic is placed squarely within a family and community constellation that might well provide an outlet for his emotional energies. Yet not only is he obsessed with objects, but he likes and dislikes others (including his wife) because of *their* relationship to things. Indeed, the authenticity, the emotional penumbra, that is absent in his relationship to others appears in his relationship to things. He gets choked up not because Melinda has given him the sweaters (he distrusts her motives and sees her as at her most dissembling when she is most "appropriately" wifelike), but because he *so likes sweaters*. They are ends in themselves. Indeed, the rapprochement with Melinda comes closest to being consummated sexually when Melinda almost accompanies Vic to his room to test the Geiger counter on Vic's conglomerate rock. It must be one of the oddest sexually charged scenes in fiction: Vic, eager to see if the rock shows any signs of radioactive heat, is at the same time anxiety stricken at the signs of his wife's sexual interest.

But if Vic relates to the world through things, Melinda relates through people. Melinda is Highsmith's most completely (if yet imperfectly) realized female character in the novels of the 1950s.[7] For the most part, Melinda is presented negatively, primarily because we always see her through Vic's (or his friends') eyes, and his thoughts of her are almost always negative: for example, her choice in men, music, but not—significantly—clothes is uniformly bad. With respect to Melinda Van Allen, Odette L'Henry Evans at first suggests the possibility of seeing "evidence of feminist self assertion, in the form of [Melinda's] determination to live life to the full."[8] But Evans eventually rejects this reading because of Melinda's lackadaisical mothering (contrasted to Vic's concerned and responsible fathering) as well as the lack of "woman's writing" in the novel, that is, "writing expressive, if even only subconsciously, of women's feelings of love and tenderness, of role-playing" (Evans, 112). But this is not the whole story. More than Miriam or Anne in *Strangers on a Train* or Marge in *The Talented Mr. Ripley,* Melinda does elicit admiration from the reader because of her absolute fearlessness in confronting and pursuing Vic; indeed, even Vic admires this quality in her. Melinda is someone who clearly knows her own mind, acts as she wishes, and does not fear the possible consequences.

The last aspect of *Deep Water* that I want to examine is its treatment of sexuality, which differs from that of the two novels previously discussed. Whereas relationships between men had a strongly homoerotic element in the earlier novels, this is not the case in *Deep Water*. Highsmith has refined the crude homoeroticism of the earlier novels into an overt asexuality on Vic's part with only the slightest suggestion of a homoerotic relationship to men below the surface. This suggestion is manifested, for example, through the way in which Vic judges Melinda's choice of men, almost at times as if he were choosing for himself. Early in the novel there is a particularly revealing instance. When Joel Nash first arrives in Little Wesley, Vic thinks he will become Melinda's next lover "because Melinda was never able to resist what she thought was a handsome face" (*Deep,* 9). Vic's implied criticism of Melinda's taste suggests that Vic has, through Melinda, a mediated relationship to her lovers. However, the homosexual motif in *Deep Water* is quite sublimated, appearing only at moments, as for example in the description of Vic's drowning De Lisle in the swimming pool, which, like Tom Ripley's murder of Dickie Greenleaf, has a sexual cast to it.

Although there are occasional flutterings of desire for Melinda on Vic's part, what he most wants is a family and to maintain appearances. One gets the feeling that under certain conditions and with an understanding woman, Vic might become sexually involved again. But Melinda is clearly not the right woman, though she was at one time, when her "animal spirits" drew Vic to her. (Indeed, one might legitimately infer that it is Vic who has changed, not Melinda, and that Melinda's affairs result from Vic's changed attitude.) Vic allows that he could see forgoing sex with Melinda for the rest of his life. What he wants is a certain closeness in terms of physical proximity and a togetherness manifested in activities such as regularly having dinner together, going on outings with Trixie, and together attending school plays. But this closeness has bounds: much is made of the fact that Vic and Melinda no longer sleep together, and it is noted several times that the living room separates their respective bedrooms. To a certain extent, Vic sees Melinda as another "tasteful" acquisition. For example, at a social event that they attend, she is acting appropriately and is not blatantly flirtatious: "She looked beautiful in a new amber-colored taffeta gown that had no belt and fitted her strong narrow waist and her hips as if it had been cut for her to the millimeter. By midnight she had danced with about fifteen partners . . . but . . . was merely pleasant and gracious to them. . . . Neither did she drink too much. Vic was extremely proud of Melinda that evening" (*Deep,* 50). For Vic, appearance and the related appropriate behavior are paramount. Vic is not interested in substance, in use value, one might say, but rather in exchange value, and Melinda's great value as a commodity is underlined by her dancing with 15 different men. Vic is satisfied with a relationship in which everything is in its place and functioning as it should, in appearance if not necessarily in substance. Although it may not be ideal—and there are occasional hints in the novel that Vic might well have liked more—he has settled for this. This is perhaps another reason for the novel's emphasis on commodities. They are the only things whose substance cannot be doubted and whose value may be easily determined. Vic's "good" taste and his Geiger counter allow him to determine the value and substance of things. He is at a distinct disadvantage when it comes to people.

Yet, deep down, Vic has real doubts as to whether even such a superficially congenial relationship is possible. Vic's tentativeness, his insecurities as well as his worldview, are all markers for the text's attempt to come to terms with domesticity and emotional closeness. The permissible amount of intimacy is spatially manifested through Melinda and Vic sleeping on opposite sides of the house, and the text is as sensitive a register of the emotional tension set off by Vic's even casual presence in Melinda's bedroom as Vic's Geiger counter is of the presence of radioactivity in his conglomerate rock. The battle that constitutes domestic life unfolds in the living room, the most frequent scene of Vic and Melinda's alcohol-pervaded domesticity.

In a strikingly poetic passage (all the more marked for the rarity with which such passages appear in Highsmith), we see Vic engaged in tending the snails he raises in aquariums in his garage.

> The snails loved the rain. He bent over one aquarium, watching the snails he called Edgar and Hortense as they slowly approached each other, lifted their heads, kissed, and glided on. They would probably mate this afternoon, in the light rain that filtered through the screen. They mated about once every week, and they were genuinely in love, Vic thought, because Edgar had eyes for no other snail but Hortense and Hortense never responded to the attempt of another snail to kiss her. Three-quarters of the thousand-odd snails he had were their progeny. They were quite considerate of each other as to which had the burden of egg-laying—a twenty-four hour procedure at least—and it was only Vic's opinion that Hortense laid more often than Edgar, which was why he had given her the feminine name. That was true love, Vic thought, even if they were only gastropoda. He remembered the sentence in one of Henri Fabre's books about snails crossing garden walls to find their mates, and though Vic had never verified it by his own experiment, he felt that it must be so. (*Deep,* 111)

Fidelity and a lack of sexual differentiation define, for Vic, the ideal conjugal relationship. The problems arising among humans from the difference that springs from sexual differentiation vanishes among the gastropoda. Difference, one might say, causes differences.

The power of *Deep Water* derives from Highsmith's depiction of the sheer inability of two people to live together, of the hell that is "others," as Sartre formulated it in his 1944 play *Huis-Clos,* and yet at the same time of the intensity of the pressure keeping them together. Anthony Boucher's suggestion of a classic dimension to the novel is not inappropriate. There is an inevitability in the fates of these two characters that is heightened—not trivialized—by the 1950s small-town setting and the text's fascination with objects. Highsmith's portrayal of the claustrophobic exurban absurd possesses an odd, compelling power.

This Sweet Sickness (1960)

This Sweet Sickness, the next novel in Highsmith's exurban trilogy, examines several of her abiding concerns: the ideal versus the material (fantasy versus reality), the family, and privacy (which, in extremis, becomes isolation). Furthermore, and as an outgrowth, elaboration, and concretization of these themes, Highsmith investigates the role of the freestanding house, perhaps the single most important constituent of the American dream. Through this theme (which appears in varying degrees in many of her novels and stories), we have, from her idiosyncratic perspective, an exploration of an issue that concerned a number of novelists at this juncture of postwar American culture.[9] Indeed, the significant role that houses play suggests a socially critical dimension to *This Sweet Sickness.*

The novel focuses on David Kelsey, a scientist employed at Cheswick Fabrics, located in a small town in the upper Hudson valley. Kelsey has refused to acknowledge the loss of his relationship with Annabelle Stanton, a woman he still loves, who has been married to Gerald Delaney for almost two years and lives with him and their baby in Hartford, Connecticut. David and Annabelle had a brief relationship before her marriage, and although David did not propose to her, he had intended to do so and is now determined to win Annabelle back. He writes her letters, attempts to start seeing her again, and refuses to admit the reality of what he terms "the Situation."[10] Indeed, although he lives in a rooming house in Froudsburg, he has (under the name of William Neumeister) bought a house outside Ballard, a small town about an hour's drive from Froudsburg. He has furnished the house in accordance with what he thinks would please Annabelle and for two years spends every weekend there, thinking of what it would be like to live there with Annabelle—in fact, fantasizing at times that she *is* there with him. He tells his fellow roomers in Froudsburg, however, that he is visiting his aged mother (who has been dead for 14 years) in a nursing home. Gerald Delaney finds out where the house is and goes there to force David to stop bothering Annabelle and himself. In the course of a scuffle, David strikes Gerald, who falls, hits his head on a stone, and dies. After the murder, David moves away from Froudsburg (and Ballard) to another city, where he finds a new job.

Before these events, however, Effie Brennan, a roomer in David's boarding house, has fallen in love with David. Although she is given no encouragement whatsoever—quite the opposite, in fact—she persists in trying to establish a relationship with him. Toward the end of the novel, she, too, is accidentally killed by David in the course of a drunken party when she and Wes Carmichael, a friend from David's job at Cheswick, pay him a visit at his new house. David then flees to New York City and, as the police close in on him, commits suicide by jumping from the eighth floor of a Riverside Drive apartment building.

The salient theme of the book is that of fantasy versus reality or, viewed in a more philosophical light, the issue of the ideal versus the material. In a number of Highsmith's novels, her protagonists, though in some ways quite bound to the real, the material (one thinks of Vic's scientific interests in *Deep Water*), succumb to fantasy to the degree that by the end of the novels their ability to distinguish between the two is impaired. Yet in *This Sweet Sickness*, David is living that unreal world from the beginning, though he is also aware of its unreality. It is not so much a descent as an intensification of something already present. Moreover, this unreal world is privileged, and it is almost as if the real world exists only to provide a take-off point for the jump into the unreal.

> His house had the tremendous virtue of never being lonely. He felt Annabelle's presence in every room. He behaved as if he were with her, even when he meditatively ate his meals. It was not like the boarding house where, with all that humanity around him he felt as lonely as an atom in space. In the pretty house Annabelle was with him, holding his hand as they listened to Bach and Brahms and Bartòk. . . .
>
> At night, he slept with her in the double bed upstairs. Her head lay on his arm, and when he turned to her and held her close, the surge of his desire had more than once reached the summit and gone over with the imagined pressure of her body, though afterward, his hand, flat against the sheet, reported only emptiness and aloneness.[11]

The passage reveals the extent to which an ideal, immaterial world is a presence for David: alone in his bed, he imagines Annabelle with him and through the force of that image has an orgasm. Yet although masturbation is what is being suggested, it is not his masturbating but rather "the *imagined* pressure of her body" that allows him to achieve orgasm. Indeed, his friend Wes later says, "If you ever got that girl, you wouldn't be able to do anything with her" (*Sweet,* 157), a remark that infuriates David.

For David, the pleasures of anticipation (a form of fantasy) at times outweigh realization. When he joins a research firm, he imagines taking part in a scientific expedition on one of its ships; after buying a book, "he unwrapped the package, looked with the pleasure of anticipation at the brand new jacket of the book" (*Sweet,* 73); a little while later, getting ready for one of his weekends, "he whistled softly to himself, anticipating the weekend which would be quieter than usual with the new fall of snow expected tonight" (*Sweet,* 77). Anticipation is a key category in Highsmith's fiction. It is important for her characters' psyches and for the reader's because it creates suspense and shifts the emphasis to the unfulfilled, the potential, the "not yet." It often results in relationships remaining sexually unconsummated. "Anticipation of the object" is one more refusal of reality. (David does not even anticipate the object—the book itself—but rather the book jacket.) Anticipation is, of course, a normal human phenomenon. But the extent to which anticipation constitutes the pleasures of her protagonists marks it in Highsmith's novels.

Whence the power fantasy possesses? For David, fantasy allows him to control his relations with others by virtually excluding them from his life. This is most evident in his relationship with Effie Brennan, who, because she is in love with David, plays the same role in their relationship as he plays with respect to Annabelle; Effie, too, will not take no for an answer. But although, like David, she acts irrationally, in her defense it must be said that at least at first, she seems merely overeager. Effie sees that David is refusing to recognize the reality that Annabelle will not ever be his and thinks that, given a chance, he may become attracted to her. In the end, however, Effie, too, remains in a fantasy world. David's refusal of others is doubly loaded in that it is ultimately a refusal of marriage and family. As in many of Highsmith's novels, marriage and family are depicted negatively. Even David's intense desire for Annabelle is open to question. Although David would seem to have wanted to marry Annabelle very much, he said nothing of marriage in the letters he wrote her daily after having moved east. Hence, unaware of his intentions and wanting to marry and raise a family, Annabelle married Gerald Delaney, whom she had known for all of a month.

Furthermore, the marriage of Wes Carmichael, David's colleague at Cheswick Fabrics, is portrayed as almost hellish. At one point, to escape his wife, Wes moves into David's rooming house without telling his wife where he has gone. Although Wes's marriage to Laura seemed briefly an idyll, "There had been a swift descent to hell, and that was the level on which Wes lived now. Often Wes visited David in the evenings to escape from Laura's tongue and from her neurotic housecleaning" (*Sweet,* 13). When the pressure of domesticity becomes too great, Wes flees his house to have drinks with David in the rooming house:

> Last Sunday he had had to shave himself at the kitchen sink, because the bathroom basin was full of combs and brushes soaking in ammonia, and the toilet was soaking [*sic*] in something else, and the tub was full of clothes. And the cleaning mops and scouring powders, the spot removers, the variously colored sponges, each for a specific purpose, the disposable toilet mops, the steel wool, the stove cleaners, the glass wax and the floor wax and the furniture wax, the Clorox and the ammonia and the silver polish that came tumbling out of the cabinet below the sink or the one in the bathroom every time he opened them. (*Sweet,* 76)

Although Wes's horrible marriage is mentioned a number of times, the description of that domestic hell does not go much beyond this. Although it seems a long list, it does not really exceed the ordinary inconveniences of living with someone, and the loss of syntactic control suggests the overdetermined quality of the passage. The 14 items (some repeated) are almost exclusively related to cleaning and are not excessive for a couple sharing a house. They are certainly no reason to leave a marriage. It would seem that the novel is reacting against the domestic situation, per se; that things get dirty and need cleaning is the force behind the hyperbolic animus of the passage.

Indeed, David's own reaction against a shared domesticity is so great that when Wes suggests that David meet Laura, his wife, David responds: "I don't want to meet her, ever. I'm sorry, Wes, but I don't" (*Sweet,* 12). And when David, in his new house, is expecting a visit from Wes, at the thought that he might be bringing Laura, he thinks: "If it was Laura . . . he simply wouldn't let them in the house" (*Sweet,* 202). But such overdetermined reactions are an integral part of Highsmith's achievement, as they not only suggest the character's irrationality but function to distance the reader from it.

The marriage and the family of Annabelle and Gerald Delaney—though they seem content—are also depicted negatively. David not only is upset that Annabelle has married someone else, someone "below her," but also is irritated by the family they have spawned. Of Hartford, where Annabelle, Gerald, and their child live, David "knew the rows of red brick houses with ten feet of space between them and that space cluttered with garbage cans and children's play wagons. He knew the flapping clotheslines and the tangle of television aerials on the roofs" (*Sweet,* 23). Things only get worse when David actually goes to Gerald and Annabelle's apartment: "He had expected clutter and the dreary appurtenances of an existence such as theirs, but the sight, the tangibleness of it all now made it far more horrible to him. There was the picture of *a hideous, gray-haired relative* on the television set beside the aerial, a pair of mole-colored house slippers in front of the armchair in whose seat lay the gaudy comic section of the Sunday newspaper. Glancing at Gerald's shoes—small, unshined—he noticed that the laces were not tied and deduced that he had interrupted Gerald in his reading" (*Sweet,* 59, italics mine). The clutter of life gets in the way of the ideal; in-laws appear, and adult intellectual stimulation is reduced to the Sunday comics. Even the description of David's work as a chemist with Cheswick Fabrics reflects the novel's antifamily animus: David's job involves developing new materials that "babies could puke on . . . just wipe them clean again with soap and water" (*Sweet,* 26).

But the most disheartening depiction of human relations is revealed through the pseudofamily of the Froudsburg rooming house. When David's landlady knocks on his door, it is because "behind her quick smile, as false as her teeth . . . she was reassuring herself once more that his room, *her* property, every thread and splinter of it, was still intact in all its ugliness. It pained David most to think that two sons who lived in St. Louis had Mrs. McCartney for a mother" (*Sweet,* 16). The 87-year-old Mrs. Beecham (whose daughter never comes to visit her) recognizes David at the door of her room: "She knew his step" (*Sweet,* 16). One gets the impression of a giant house continuously eavesdropping on itself, allowing no one any privacy. The family, fellow boarders at the rooming house, colleagues at work—people—are always prying, intrusive, ultimately aggressing.

Moreover, and perhaps even more depressing than the animate occupants of the rooming house, are its objects. At dinner one evening, "David stared at a dingy painting of a north woods landscape on the wall in front of him, looked at the corner cupboard with its hideous display of thick white mugs and a few plates, all from the dime store. The wall paper was light blue, but not uniformly blue. Its pale sections showed the shapes of pictures and pieces of furniture that had blocked out the light for years" (*Sweet,* 38–39). The animus revealed in this description exceeds anything rooted in reality, and nothing in the numerous domestic scenes depicted in the novel justifies the intense reaction against domesticity that David (and Wes) indulge in. But this over-the-top quality gives the novel a compelling power. Although novelists such as John Updike (*Rabbit, Run,* 1960) and Philip Roth (*Letting Go,* 1962) depicted failed relationships and, in the case of the Updike novel, a flight from domesticity, those were in the nature of case studies, which, taken together, might be interpreted as saying something about the changes marriage was undergoing as the 1950s became the 1960s. But those novels did not depict the institution as so irreparably problematic as does *This Sweet Sickness.* What is so powerful about Highsmith's novel is the irrational intensity of David Kelsey's reaction to what is, after all, normal domestic life and—even more—the intensity of the fantasy that he establishes to counteract it.

All this is changed utterly in Ballard, where David has solved the problem of other people by isolating himself from them in a house under his control, which he furnishes with ideal objects and peoples with an ideal object of his love. Here David spends his weekends, preparing his meals and puttering about, "installing a wall lamp. . . . It was a special kind of lamp that he had ordered from a New York department store by mail" (*Sweet,* 20). He is completely at ease: "He moved very smoothly and happily, more smoothly and far more happily than he did at Mrs. McCartney's or at the factory" (*Sweet,* 20). The contrast between the furnishings of the house (where positional goods play an important role) and the rooming house (where commodities reign) could not be more striking.[12] One Sunday, David "played some Haydn on the phonograph and drifted about his house, looking at the backs of his art books, at his framed manuscript page of a Beethoven theme which had cost him a considerable sum, at the gold-leaf-framed Leonardo drawing which had cost more, and at his silver tea set on a table in a corner of the living room, which he realized with a little shame he had never used once" (*Sweet,* 56–57). "Drifted" is striking and an admirable choice here. David is like a fish, swimming among his possessions. In fact, David's private, hermetically sealed-off environment resembles an aquarium, definitively cut off from contact with the outside world, and just as one buys accessories to place in an aquarium, so David buys his things with a view to where they will go and how they will look in his rarefied environment. The fish is in and of its environment, and so is David, constituting that Sartrean "possessor-possessed" unity (which I will discuss) that forms the ultimate goal of possession. Indeed, David's slight pang at the realization that the tea set has not been used would seem to confirm Sartre's statement that "it is only when I pass beyond *my* objects toward a goal, when I utilize them, that I can enjoy their possession" (Sartre, 754).

David has bought and furnished the house for Annabelle, and it represents a significant element of his character and way of thinking. This element, although present in many of Highsmith's protagonists, is most clearly delineated with respect to David. It derives from that special relationship that Highsmith's characters have with things, and in the end, it sometimes undoes them. David cannot understand why Annabelle does not immediately reject the messy clutter of her Hartford life and come to live with him in exurban comfort. He sees his good taste and ability to provide Annabelle with nice things as prima facie evidence that theirs would be a successful marriage. It is almost as if David views human relationships as something like an algebraic equation with a number of unknowns. Once the correct values—that is, objects—for those unknowns are found, the equation is solved. In this case, Annabelle will throw over Gerald and marry David once the house has been filled with the proper values. David sees himself in this way. He functions more smoothly in his house, surrounded by the proper things, "more smoothly and far more happily than he did at Mrs. McCartney's" (*Sweet,* 20). But the quality that appeals to David about objects, that they can be controlled, eludes him in his relationships with people. He cannot control Effie in her desire for him, nor Annabelle, who has married someone else. It is hard to see how a relationship with Annabelle would have escaped this dilemma. In the end, David is a solipsist unable to acknowledge anyone but himself.

David has constructed his life in the house to sanitize his imagined relationship with Annabelle, not wanting to have it sullied by any connection with the grubby atmosphere of the rooming house. Hence, he has taken his house under the assumed name of William Neumeister, and even remarks on the facile irony of the English translation of that name, "new-master," though it appeals to him nonetheless. After Gerald is killed, David continues to maintain the separate Neumeister identity, even returning to Ballard as Neumeister to talk to the police. His behavior is reminiscent of Tom Ripley in *The Talented Mr. Ripley*, when Ripley switched back and forth several times between his own identity and impersonating Dickie Greenleaf. Yet in that instance, Ripley had good reason for continuing the impersonation, as it enabled him to receive Dickie's money. In *This Sweet Sickness,* no such reason exists. Nor is it a question of averting any legal guilt because the police accept the events as they are described, and in fact, David had no intention of killing Gerald.

The attraction of maintaining a separate personality can be traced to the same root as the appeal of the isolated house, of the ideal relationship with Annabelle, and also resembles Tom Ripley's project of fashioning himself. In a world as purely objectified as that which David envisions, he desires to create himself by possessing objects, and he would like Annabelle to be one more such possession. The phenomenon of possession was analyzed by Sartre in a way that clarifies David's relationship to objects and to people. "The desire of a particular object," Sartre writes, "is not the simple desire *of* this object; it is the desire to be united with the object in an internal relation" (Sartre, 751). Sartre aptly summarizes what could be a definition of this relationship for David: "The totality of my possessions reflects the totality of my being. I *am* what I have. It is I myself which I touch in this cup, in this trinket" (Sartre, 755). The unity of "possessor-possessed" that Sartre sees as the goal of such a relationship is revealed through David's inability to distinguish between himself and others, the other pole of his drive for isolation, illustrated by his vowing to do anything for Annabelle or, on the other hand, his revulsion at those objects—symbolized by the rooming house—with which he cannot bear being united. He imagines that if he can seal himself off with the desired possessions, the perfect relationship can be created. But once he comes into contact with messy, material existence, all is lost. The attempt to keep William Neumeister separate is an attempt to retain this ideal, unsullied existence, an attempt to materialize the ideal.

An important feature of the novel is the relationship between Effie Brennan and David Kelsey. It is, in fact, more of an actual relationship than that between David and Annabelle. Yet it is even more ill-fated and both underlines the novel's pessimistic view of relationships and provides another example of humanity's inability to face reality. Although she suspects David may be seeing another woman, Effie does not believe him when he tells Effie he is engaged. "You know, I just don't believe that story. Wes told me too, but that just isn't the way things are" (*Sweet,* 107). This moment nicely captures Effie's dilemma. On the one hand, her instincts about David are right. She realizes that

David's only "involvement" is his neurotic, imaginary one with Annabelle. Effie sees that it would be to his advantage to free himself from
this and to get on with his life. Hence, she feels there is a chance for herself. Yet at the same time, her overdetermined involvement with him
prevents her from seeing the extent of his pathology.

Yet one forgives Effie her irrationality. David is depicted as an attractive man and is seen as such by coworkers and the boarding-house society. He is a professional scientist and makes a good living ($25,000 a
year in 1958). In the small town, one can understand the attraction he
represents for Effie and why she is so reluctant to give him up. Hence,
Effie's continued pursuit of David is more rational than David's of
Annabelle. When Effie last visits David, in his new house near Troy, it is
after she has learned that Annabelle has remarried following Gerald's
death. Hence, she feels she is justified in giving it one more shot with
David. The visit, however, ends in her death, which occurs in a vague
clause as he "thrust her from him" (*Sweet,* 212). But though there may
be a certain tactical rationality to Effie's behavior, from a wider angle
she, too, acts irrationally.

Although David has much in common with Vic Van Allen in *Deep
Water,* Effie has only her ultimate fate as victim in common with
Melinda Van Allen. Effie's somewhat clinging relationship to David is
the opposite of Melinda's determined independence. Yet they both meet
the same fate: death at the hands of the male protagonist. Highsmith
has constructed an odd emotional magnetic field in which the strongest
force uniting people is repulsion. Although it might seem at first glance,
especially because of the intensity of David's attraction to Annabelle,
that this is not the case, on closer examination, it is repulsion that determines the various vectors in the novels; negativity is the lodestone of the
characters' interpersonal dynamics. David's strongest emotions express
his displeasure at Effie's pursuit. When, packing up his Ballard house,
David realizes that it is Effie in a car that has stopped outside, and
bursts out "Jesus!" (*Sweet,* 105), the reader feels the release of tension as
one of the most explosive moments in the novel. David's "thrusting
Effie from him" can be taken as paradigmatic of his relation to people
and to the world generally and perfectly symbolizes the search for a privacy verging on isolation and for control that runs so strongly through
the novel.

David Kelsey's world in *This Sweet Sickness* is perhaps the most perfectly private, the most hermetically sealed, of any in Highsmith. Not
one of her other protagonists seems so bereft of social ties, so much the

prisoner of fantasy. Hence, it might at first seem unjustified to speak of a socially critical aspect to the novel. Yet the very extremity of the character and his world suggests such a discussion. Although I do not want simplistically to analogize David Kelsey's situation to the situation of late-1950s America, I do think there is a sense in which Highsmith's fictional world represents a kind of America in extremis, a perverse realization of some mainstream tendencies in American life. The freestanding house, which David Kelsey buys two of in the course of this relatively short novel, becomes a dominant theme. The house that David desires is not a quasi row house like the one in which Annabelle lives in Hartford, with barely 10 feet separating it from its neighbor, but a house *a mile* from any other house. For David, the atomization of society has become so complete that the idea of neighbors is anathema. Whereas neighbors inhabit the classic suburban vision (as in the short stories of John Cheever, for example), David has—and desires—no neighbors. Nor is there a positive vision of the small town. Froudsburg—with its diner, its bar, its dance hall (of which, significantly, David was not even aware), and above all its rooming house—is creepy. (The name of the town, with its suggestion of both frowning and dowdy, is particularly apt.) Froudsburg does not even possess the attractive underlay of sinful desire that runs through Anderson's *Winesburg, Ohio*. Moreover, David and Annabelle met in La Jolla, California, and hence their current residence in the East suggests that the West no longer functions as a possible refuge. Even New York, attractive though it seems with its upscale amusements, its attractive commodities, is merely the place where David leaps to his death as he holds on to his fantasy: "[T]hinking no more about it, he stepped off into that cool space, that fast descent to her, with nothing in his mind but a memory of a curve of her shoulder, naked, as he had never seen it" (*Sweet,* 250). Highsmith has not written a novel of social criticism. This was never, not even in the 1970s, her primary concern. Yet the overwhelming barrenness and the claustrophobic nature of David Kelsey's world and the sterility of the vision of life presented in *This Sweet Sickness* suggest a critical perspective. There is not even the slightest suggestion of a more positive alternative, neither for the individual nor for society.

The Cry of the Owl (1962)

The Cry of the Owl continues the exploration of small-town domesticity begun in *Deep Water*. It continues, as well, though in more subdued form, the exploration of fantasy that played so prominent a part in *This Sweet Sickness*. But in a peculiarly subtle and oblique way, it also touches on the issue of political persecution, although its presence is so shadowy that it is unlikely to draw the reader's immediate attention.

The novel is set in Langley, a small town in eastern Pennsylvania, where Robert Forester, an engineer working on helicopter design at Langley Aeronautics, has fled his relationship with his wife, Nickie. (Their divorce takes effect during the first pages of the novel.) He becomes involved with Jenny Thierolf, whom he has taken to spying on in the isolated house where she lives by herself. Their acquaintance begins after she finally spots him and invites him inside. Jenny has been unenthusiastically engaged to Greg Wyncoop but breaks off the engagement, a decision Greg refuses to accept, believing Robert has alienated Jenny's affections. Greg becomes upset and at one point assaults Robert in a lonely spot by a river. Robert gets the best of him, but Greg then disappears, hoping through the appearance of his death (a body has been found washed up by the river) to implicate Robert as his murderer. Greg is befriended by Robert's ex-wife, Nickie (with whom he has a brief affair), while hiding out in New York City and on three further occasions attempts to kill Robert. Greg fails each time, though he kills a neighbor's dog Robert has befriended, twice wounds him, and in the last attempt, kills a kindly old doctor who has befriended Robert. Greg is apprehended toward the end of the novel but is released on bail, and the novel ends on a grotesque note as Greg accidentally stabs Nickie to death in a fight with Robert.

This bizarre and intense plot provides the vehicle for Highsmith's examination of the various themes I have discussed. The novel seems to me one of Highsmith's best, and although it has occasionally been recognized as such, I think it has also suffered in critical appreciation because of its similarity to its immediate predecessor.[13] Yet it is different enough to warrant close attention, and to my mind, by virtue of its shadowy suggestion of a political moment, begins to explore an area that was to become more prominent in Highsmith's fiction toward the end of the decade.

The most striking aspect of the novel is the creation of the relationship between Robert Forester and Jenny Thierolf through what is always described as Robert's "prowling." The manner in which the relationship is begun not only determines the course of the novel but also functions as a touchstone for the issue of domestic interpersonal relations. Both Robert's choice of prowling as a way to begin the relationship and the function prowling fills in his "domestic economy" are crucial for this issue, and the prowling also serves as the link to politics.

Jenny lives in an isolated house on a gravel road off a main road, and Robert has to drive up, park, and walk to where he can spy on her without being seen (especially because he does his prowling toward the evening). The "fourth or fifth time" he engages in this activity, "the girl was in the kitchen again. Its two squares of light showed at the back of the house, and now and again her figure crossed one of the squares, but stayed mostly in the left square, where the table was. To Robert's view, the window was like the tiny focus of a camera. He did not always go closer to the house. He was very much afraid of being seen by her."[14] "To Robert," purely an observer, "she was all of a piece, like a properly made statue" (*Cry*, 10). Robert is satisfied with watching her anonymously, viewing her as an especially appropriate piece of kitchen equipment, and does not follow her to find out where she works because "his pleasure in watching her, he realized, was very much connected with the house. He liked her domesticity, liked to see her take pleasure in putting up curtains and hanging pictures. He liked best to watch her pottering about in the kitchen" (*Cry*, 11).

Robert is trying Jenny out, as it were, to see if she might fit into his fantasy of perfect domesticity, and throughout the novel, he remains ambivalent toward her. After she falls in love with him, he almost, but not quite, rejects her. He can never say for sure whether they will be right for each other; that is, he does not know if he can ever love Jenny the way she loves him and therefore refuses to have sex with her. Of course, anyone contemplating marriage in a Highsmith novel is treading on thin ice, and this novel is no exception. Its roster of marriages does not suggest a sanguine view of the institution. Robert's mother has divorced Robert's father (of whom we know only that he drank too much) and remarried (the first time Robert is shot by Greg, his answering a phone call from his mother has made him a stationary target). Jenny's parents are a sad-looking couple; one of their sons died of spinal meningitis, and their daughter, Jenny, eventually commits suicide. Robert's best friend at work, Jack Nielson, lives in straitened circumstances because he and his wife support a pair of aged in-laws. Greg Wyncoop's father is prematurely aged—his one son is an alcoholic failure, and his other son, Greg, is a murderer. And, as one critic wrote, Nickie, Robert's ex-wife, is a "dangerous psychopath. . . . an almost schizophrenic hysteric."[15]

However, Robert's ambivalence has two roots. The first has to do with the preference of Highsmith's characters for living their lives in a fantasy world of anticipation, which will always be spoiled by any kind of concrete realization. This dynamic is reflected by Robert's continually edging away from Jenny as she attempts to get closer to him while he has second thoughts about his edging away as she withdraws from him. The first time Jenny becomes aware of him watching her, she, with some hesitation, invites him in, but "his pleasure or satisfaction in seeing her more closely now was no greater than when he had looked at her through the window, and he foresaw that getting to know her even slightly would be to diminish her and what she stood for to him—happiness and calmness and the absence of any kind of strain" (*Cry*, 30–31).

But the second dynamic is equally important and a corollary of the first. It derives from the tendency of Highsmith's protagonists to objectify (and at times to commodify) other people in order to control their mutual relations. Robert, who has just escaped from a horribly destructive marriage, is trying somehow to determine—*in advance*—whether this woman will fit in the scene of domesticity that he projects for himself, exercising the penchant for control that provides a significant component of the psychological gain derived from fantasy. Hence, Robert is quite careful before he literally enters the domestic minefield a second time, wanting to control as closely as possible the variables involved. Thus, even before he truly meets Jenny, he has reified her ("she was all of a piece, like a properly made statue" [*Cry*, 10]) and placed her in her role in the domestic scene, "pottering about in the kitchen." Indeed, invited inside at that first meeting, he thinks to himself: "[H]ere, so near he could touch them, were the white curtains he had seen her put up, the oven door he had seen her so often bend to open" (*Cry*, 30), as if the objects are more important than the person. Although both the preference for the unrealized and the desire for control were present in *This Sweet Sickness,* there are significant differences in the way Highsmith explores these themes in *The Cry of the Owl.*

The most important difference is that Robert Forester's behavior is well within normal limits, whereas David Kelsey's fantasy of domestic life had a lunatic edge from the very beginning;[16] moreover, Jenny's interest in Robert is not at all unrealistic and is even slightly encouraged by him and thus differs both from David Kelsey's irrational pursuit of Annabelle Stanton as well as from Effie Brennan's passion for Kelsey. What is similar is the privileging of fantasy in both novels. This derives from, and at the same time intensifies, the subjective aspect of Highsmith's characters. With very little exception, these individuals live in their own worlds and, in the more extreme cases, cannot recognize a social world.

Greg Wyncoop is yet another example of this intense subjectivity. After he has shot at Robert on three separate occasions, Greg winds up killing the kindly old Dr. Knott, who has taken Robert into his house specifically to protect him from further murder attempts: because Dr. Knott's house has a second story, it is less likely that Greg will have a good shot at Robert. Before being released from jail, Greg thinks of the reaction of his boss and family: "Alex was going to act like a self-righteous holier than thou, too, Greg supposed. Let them rail at him, let them lecture him, what did he care? He hadn't done anything wrong enough to be clapped in jail for. It was ridiculous" (*Cry*, 226). There is something almost infantile (or at best adolescent) about Greg's inability to see beyond his own self. Robert Forester's reactions also verge on the solipsistic at times. Although he often wonders about how others—usually Jenny—will react to what he says or does, the obsessively self-involved quality of these ruminations belies their apparent concern for others. But the extreme subjectivity, or interiority, present in *The Cry of the Owl* has distinct, if disguised, social roots. It suggests, as in the instances cited, a refusal to recognize a social world, any value higher than that of the individual. It is as if we see the image of the 1950s as a quiescent, self-satisfied decade reflected in a fun-house mirror.

Personalizing the Political/Politicizing the Personal

An important theme in *The Cry of the Owl* concerns the behavior of Robert's friends and neighbors and the community at large as Greg's continued absence casts suspicion on Robert. It is known that the two men have fought and that Greg had fallen into the river. Although Robert has told the police that he pulled Greg from the river and left him on the bank, alive, the appearance of a washed-up corpse and Greg's absence lead more and more people to suspect that Robert is lying and that he murdered Greg. The police, too, harbor such suspicions. Hence no one seems to take Robert very seriously when he says that it is Greg who is shooting at him. As a result of Greg's first attempt, Robert suffers a slight wound, and a stray dog he has fed is killed during the attack. As Robert calls the police, "in walked a tall, gray-haired man in work clothes, his mouth half-open in bewilderment. It was Kolbe, his next-door neighbor. . . . The man was looking at the dog, frowning, bending over it. 'That's the *Huxmeyer's* dog,' he said in an angry tone" (*Cry*, 180). It is an unexpected, absurd, and even frightening reaction, so unexpected and inappropriate that the reader is prevented from making any conventional sense of such behavior. Someone has tried to kill Robert, and his neighbor blames him for a dog's death. The two opposing views are so irreconcilable in their antagonistic perspectives that the reader feels that the two people inhabit different universes.

Yet it is not just another individual that Robert is up against, but the entire community, eager to convict him of something he did not do and of which he has not even been accused, let alone tried. The persecutory zeal of the mob is clear when after the police have arrived, one of the bystanders reacts: " 'He killed a man, didn't he?' screamed the woman called Martha" to which "a couple of people, quietly, in unison" respond "Yes" (*Cry*, 182). A little later, Dr. Knott (the man of science and traditional representative of reason in such situations) tells the police to ask the people to leave the house, and Robert thinks to himself: "The voice of reason, the small voice of reason was speaking up. One against thirteen or fourteen, or maybe it was twenty" (*Cry*, 183).

Because the reader identifies with Robert, knowing that Greg attacked Robert first, is alive, and has been trying to murder him, the community appears as a collection of prejudiced, irrational, witch-hunting individuals, more than willing to suspect Robert merely because he is an outsider and has been rumored to have seduced Jenny and in any event has alienated her affections from Greg.[17] The truth is that Robert and Jenny are not lovers, and Jenny no longer has any interest in marrying Greg and was never, in any event, all that keen on him. As the instances of Robert's persecution by the community mount, there is a distinctly overdetermined quality to the ways in which these injustices are presented, and the reader gradually but inevitably begins to sense that something else is going on.[18] It seems to me that Highsmith has constructed something like an allegorical tale of the witch-hunt, of the blacklist, in short, of McCarthyism. Although there is no mention of this subject, and such an interpretation might seem far-fetched, if looked at from this perspective, it explains much of the community's behavior in *The Cry of the Owl*.

One important technique in the practice of McCarthyite persecution was the idea of guilt by association: association with Communists, for example, was used to suggest you were a Communist (not illegal in any event). Although you might not actually be a member of the Communist Party, if your ideas overlapped at all with the party's, then you were as good as a member or at best a fellow traveler. Attending a meeting with Communists, reading a leftist book, or supporting a program the Communists also supported was as damning as being a member of the

Party; the Party was seen as un-American. Another technique was to inflate suspicion into conviction of the full-blown deed itself, for example, spying for the Russians. Above all was the use of hearsay, rumor, and appearance to declare guilt.

Robert's original "crime" of prowling is blown up by the community into his conviction as a Peeping Tom who has seduced Jenny. In the novel, this conviction carries the weight of membership in the Communist Party, and Robert is an outsider ("foreign") to the community, hence easily viewed as a "spy" (prowling is a form of spying). Indeed, Robert, who works for an aeronautics firm (a defense-related job where he might well be working on projects vital to national security), feels that his reputation as a prowler has just about cost him his job and that he might as well resign and move to another city. But Robert is falsely accused: he was not looking at Jenny as a Peeping Tom, nor has he seduced her, though he is somewhat attracted to her. But as an outsider to the community (i.e., "un-American"), he is suspect a priori. The same falseness holds for his "seduction" of Jenny. Although Jenny has slept at Robert's a few times, he has refused to have sex with her (though she seemed willing). From this fact, the community has convicted him of seducing her. The prowling has been taken for evidence of his perversion, just as the support of liberal causes was taken as proof of being a Communist; the prowling is metaphorical membership in a front group for perversion. But most important is that the community has rushed to judge Robert a murderer, assuming that because he had a reason to kill Greg (his rival, they think, for Jenny's affections), he did kill Greg. The hostile bystander goes on to shout at Robert, "And you deserve it! You deserve it!" to which are added "a few grunts of approval among the people." "He killed a man, didn't he?" she "screamed" (*Cry,* 182).

A little later Robert decides to quit his job at Langley Aeronautics. "As soon as I can, I'm going to write a letter resigning. Quitting. I'm licked. It's true" (*Cry,* 192), he tells his friend and colleague, Jack Nielson. The tone is very much that of a man who has battled for a political cause but has been pressed beyond endurance by a benighted, bigoted community. Yet such a tone is inappropriate to the actual events, which have no overt political content. The incongruity between the tone of Robert's reaction to the events and the events themselves and the hectoring, accusatory tone of the neighbors suggests a covert reference to the politics of the witch-hunt.

There is a further point to be made. It relates not only to *The Cry of the Owl* but to *This Sweet Sickness* and to *Deep Water* as well. What I want to suggest is that there is a level on which the extremely self-involved, sometimes solipsistic nature of Highsmith's protagonists has a political dimension. In its extreme fixation on the isolated self, such behavior represents both a reaction to the failure of the social and literary movements of the 1930s and early 1940s as well as a criticism of this very withdrawal into the self—the retreat to the individual, *tout court*—characteristic of the decade from the early 1950s to the early 1960s.

These novels enact and critique this phenomenon. It is of more than idiosyncratic significance that David Kelsey, Robert Forester, and Jenny Thierolf all construct for themselves isolated existences removed from the social world. This isolation is nowhere so forcefully represented as in the virtually instinctive drive that these characters possess for living alone, in a house, in the woods. None of them want to live alone; they are all interested in forming a couple (although their interest does not extend to reproduction); and in the cases of David and Jenny, this desire leads to their death. Indeed, they are sometimes drawn more by the form than by the content of such a union. As Robert Forester says to Jenny: "Life is meaningless unless you're living it for some other person. I was living for you since September—*even though I didn't know you*" (33, my emphasis). Yet, driven by their unrealizable fantasies, none of them can ever materialize their desire. The problems Highsmith's characters encounter in doing this, and their highly subjective world, are not just functions of their individual psyches but also a concrete manifestation of a retreat from the socially committed world of the 1930s and early 1940s. The retreat into the world of the isolated individual depicted in these novels thus becomes—against the grain to be sure—a socially critical moment in the novels by virtue of its failure.

The tendency of Highsmith's characters—here Robert Forester, but Vic Van Allen also has such moments—to see themselves as in some sense "heroic" is a result of this displacement of the latent social aspect onto the individual. An essential element of heroism is the willingness to sacrifice oneself for something greater than the self. That the protagonists so often see themselves as heroic suggests that the dynamic behind the heroic self-image has been displaced from the social onto the personal.[19]

Chapter Four
Politics in the Novels

If Highsmith began the 1960s with an intensive examination of the domestic relations of Americans, by the decade's end, she had begun to explore U.S. foreign relations and political and social issues generally. Such issues began to loom large in her work. But a new problem arose. In investigating issues such as the United States' role as a neoimperialist power in Southeast Asia and the anti–Vietnam War movement at home, and later in the decade the status of women, her approach to these issues was hindered in two not-unrelated ways. First, by taking up permanent residence abroad in 1963, when public life (formal politics, the civil rights movement, the antiwar movement) and private life (the counterculture) were undergoing radical change, as was the relationship between the two, she was cut off from the direct relationship to such movements that can intimately affect a writer's work. And although there are advantages as well as disadvantages to the distance of the expatriate, her European vantage point (even granting her occasional trips to the United States) made for a somewhat stilted representation of American society. In addition, Highsmith's roots were in the United States of the 1930s through the 1950s, and the radical rupture in American politics and culture effected by the 1960s meant that those roots were now glaringly exposed, her prior four decades of American experience become something of a stumbling block to interpreting the events of this radical break. At the same time, the decision to broaden the scope of her novels to include social and political issues had interesting consequences, not only on the novels themselves—but on our assessment of her earlier work.

The Tremor of Forgery (1969)

The Tremor of Forgery is one of Highsmith's best-received novels and was something like a watershed in her career. It was the least marked of her novels since *The Price of Salt* and has distinct political overtones. From this point on, roughly half of her novels would be what we might call "unmarked."[1] Perhaps as a result (although cause and effect are not easy to disentangle here), her subsequent novels would concern themselves with political and social issues far more than did her earlier work.

The novel is set in Tunisia around the time of the 1967 Arab-Israeli Six Days' War. Howard Ingham, a New York novelist and scriptwriter, has come to Tunisia to prepare for a film he will write, which is to be shot in the country with a friend. Ingham meets a retired American expatriate, Francis Adams, with whom Ingham forms a casual friendship, and Anders Jensen, a Danish painter living in Tunisia, who becomes a closer friend. Soon after Ingham's arrival, he learns that John Castlewood, the film's director, has committed suicide in New York. When Ina Pallant, Ingham's fiancée, arrives, she tells him that she had a brief affair with Castlewood and that he committed suicide after learning that Ina would not give up Ingham for him.

About a third of the way into the novel, a crucial event occurs, defining Ingham's relationship to each of the others and revealing the novel's political dimension. Ingham has been living in a bungalow belonging to a large hotel in the resort of Hammamet, where local Arabs are known to commit petty thefts from unlocked cars and bungalows. One night Ingham hears someone opening his door. Suspecting a burglar, he picks up his metal typewriter and hurls it at the invisible intruder. The typewriter strikes the intruder, who groans and falls down outside the bungalow. Ingham then locks the door. Soon workers from the hotel carry away the body and clean up any blood that may have been spilled. Although a local Arab, Abdullah, is suspected, the reader never learns whether he was the intruder, whether the intruder was killed, or, in fact, anything further about the incident. Eventually, Francis Adams suspects it was Ingham who injured the intruder. Ingham, however, does not admit to anything other than having been awakened by some noise. When Ina arrives, she is eventually affected by Adams's doubt and pressures Ingham to disclose what happened. Eventually he does, but with this admission comes the loss of any desire to marry Ina, who returns to New York alone. Ingham remains in Tunisia, finishing up a novel, and returns to New York a few days later, heartened by a cordial letter from his ex-wife, about whom he has begun to think more positively.

Ingham is the nexus of the novel, and his relationship with Adams, Pallant, and Jensen, as well as his involvement in the possible murder of Abdullah, provides the novel's focus. The novel is narrated from his point of view and suggests thematic literary connections (one of which is quite important ideologically) to two earlier novels, Gide's *The Immoralist* (1902) and Camus's *The Stranger* (1942), that deal with the relationship of Europeans to Africa and, in a broader sense, to the Third World. But it is the radically different manner in which Highsmith treats the analogous moments linking her novel to her predecessors' that is worth noting, and I will discuss this later in this section. Last, there is here a confrontation between the irrationalist-existentialist, quasi-absurdist themes of Highsmith's novels of the 1950s and the realities of shifting global politics of the 1960s, most immediately the 1967 Arab-Israeli war and, more importantly, the crises within and outside the United States, manifested in the civil unrest resulting from the civil rights movement, and, paramount with respect to *The Tremor of Forgery*, the fissure created in American society by the Vietnam War. These crises are continually explored in discussions between Ingham and Adams and in the relations between the novel's European and Arab characters.

There are various conflicts in the book, and much of the novel's fascination lies in the strategy it employs to resolve them. Ideologically, it is one of Highsmith's least stable novels (and this instability reflects its historical moment), although formally it is her most controlled book, a quality that has led a number of readers to consider it her best.[2] From this fission of unstable content and stabilizing form results a linguistic fallout that I find to be one of the most striking aspects of the novel: an almost pathological literalness and reliance on detail. Although the obsession with detail had a strong presence in Highsmith's previous texts, it remained under control or was incorporated thematically. In *The Tremor of Forgery,* it threatens to get out of control.

The three principal male characters occupy that peculiar Highsmithian space that exists just outside the main socioeconomic currents of contemporary life. Anders Jensen's trust fund allows him to live and paint where he wants; Francis Adams is a retiree proselytizing for the American way of life who has been living in Tunisia for a year, engaged in what may be privately supported illegal propaganda broadcasts to Eastern Europe; and Howard Ingham is a moderately successful novelist and scriptwriter who has received $50,000 for his most recent movie script. Moreover, they are further isolated in that Adams and Jensen have expatriated themselves to North Africa, and although Ingham is, presumably, in Tunisia for a limited time, he begins to contemplate a longer stay. Furthermore, because they are foreigners, they have little to do with Tunisian society beyond their contact with the small number of natives serving them.[3] Indeed, although the setting is that of a North African beach resort in summer, with its physical expanse of beach, sea, and desert, the emotional atmosphere is as claustrophobic as any in Highsmith.

The novel's ideological instability stems in part from Ingham's ambivalence. Although the obvious connection to *The Immoralist* suggests the question of sexual orientation, Ingham's (and the novel's) most evident ambivalence has to do with politics. Although Adams, Jensen, and Pallant harbor no doubts about their views, Ingham is often at a loss as to how to interpret, judge, and react to events. Because we view the events of the novel through his consciousness, it may seem natural to take him as the author's spokesperson; yet there is enough contrary evidence to show that this would be a mistake. In the discrepancy, in fact, lie the politics of the novel. Ingham is the focus for the conflicting conclusions we draw.

Like many of Highsmith's protagonists, his is none too fixed a personality. His profession of novelist and scriptwriter places him in the world of the creative professional. Yet his lack of attachment to any institution allows him to float in that vaguely defined space that gives him a limited autonomy. The fact that he has received $50,000 for the screen rights to his last novel grants him a limited economic freedom and suggests society's positive valuation of his work. Personal relationships hover in the same pleasantly cloudy state: he is engaged, in a way, to—though not madly in love with—Ina Pallant, a script supervisor for ABC TV. Ina is the only person in the novel who has a real job, and this structures the novel, as her time in Tunisia is limited by the demands of her work. If she did not have to return to New York by a fixed date, Ingham would not have to decide about his feelings for her, a decision that is crucial in resolving the problems that have arisen for him.

Furthermore, another aspect of this novel that differs markedly from the earlier novels also effects a change in the position of the protagonist: here, nothing illegal or apparently illegal has happened. Beginning with *A Suspension of Mercy* (1965) and continuing through *Those Who Walk Away* (1967), Highsmith began to shift plot events from crimes to possibly criminal acts to, as in *The Tremor of Forgery,* the absence of crime. We do not know that a murder has been committed, and even if Ingham has killed Abdullah, it seems unlikely that he would have been charged with a crime because he was acting in self-defense against a nighttime intruder. In fact, the vague and tricky character of the events of that night and the difficulty of judging Ingham's subsequent behavior not only provide the core of the novel's action but—for the same reasons—allow us to see how these events stand in for the latent political content of the novel.

The crucial event occurs when Ingham is awakened one night and hears his doorknob turning.

He saw silhouetted a somewhat stooped figure; a light . . . gave a milky luminosity beyond. The figure was coming in.

Ingham seized his typewriter from the table and hurled it with all his force, shoving it with his right arm in the manner of a basket-ball player throwing for the basket—but in this case the target was lower. Ingham scored a direct hit against the turbaned head. The typewriter fell with a painful clatter, and there was a yell from the figure which staggered back and fell on the terrace. Ingham sprang to his door, pushed the typewriter aside with one foot, and slammed the door. (*Tremor*, 94)

Ingham hears people drag the body off and sweep away any signs of what has happened. Ingham is "ninety per cent sure" that the man was Abdullah, a local Arab who has stolen things out of unlocked cars and whom Ingham has seen suspiciously hanging around his car and his bungalow. Ingham does not report the incident to anyone at the hotel or to the police and at first tells only Jensen about it. Jensen, who places little value on an Arab's life, advises Ingham to forget about the incident as a matter of no consequence. Adams eventually suspects Ingham, though Ingham never admits the truth to him. The event and Ingham's subsequent behavior form the novel's problematic, and Highsmith's exploration of the characters' various responses and our reactions as readers effect at the same time a consideration of larger political issues.

The nexus for this politicization is the assault and possible murder of an Arab by a westerner. This constellation inevitably evokes Camus's 1942 novel *The Stranger,* one of the most important novels of the past 50 years and in the 1950s and 1960s a basic text for the discussion of the existentialist *acte gratuit* and the absurd.[4] The crucial moment of Camus's novel is the European colonist's apparently gratuitous murder of an Arab. The differences in Camus's and Highsmith's treatment of the murder of an Arab by a westerner reflect significant historical events of the 27 years between the two novels. But the treatment of the political issues also reflects Highsmith's position as a representative of a formally noncolonialist power suffering internal divisions over its neoimperialist project in Vietnam. In Camus's novel, the murder was presented as unmotivated in any conventional sense. Hence, there are two important differences: in Highsmith we are never sure that a murder has been committed. Second, the assault is quite motivated, as Ingham was consciously trying to harm (though not necessarily kill) the intruder. What remains the same is that in both cases a European has assaulted a non-European native. Moreover, although the different historical eras frame the events differently (in 1942 Algeria was a French *Départment,* whereas in 1967 Tunisia was an independent country), the value of a non-European life remains the issue.[5]

This last point is the most important element in the situation because it is what effects the connection with the larger issue of the Vietnam War. Shortly after the incident, Ingham thinks to himself: "And what was the Arab worth? Next to nothing, probably" (*Tremor,* 101). Later, taking an overnight camel trip into the desert with Jensen to visit an oasis, "The camels looked more intelligent than their drivers, Ingham thought" (*Tremor,* 119–20). Although it would be a mistake to identify such thoughts with the author (they are, for one thing, too blatantly racist to evoke much in the way of assent from the reader), there are more subtle ways in which the event is both trivialized and problematized, some more closely under authorial control, others perhaps not. First, there is the sense in which Camus is being parodied. This derives from the increased problematization due to the different historical context as well as the somewhat "naive" original reception of Camus's novel. In *The Stranger,* the Arab is killed with a gun pointed directly at his head; in Highsmith's novel, a typewriter is thrown at the intruder, we do not know if anyone is killed, and we do not know for certain that the victim is an Arab. The cause of the assault was an attempt at petty burglary, and the Arabs themselves, rather than demanding prosecution, hush up the incident. This muddying of waters mirrors, I think, the ambivalent response of mainstream American society to the U.S. involvement in Vietnam (where, it is worth noting, the United States was the direct imperial successor to the French). This confusion determines Ingham's subsequent behavior: his failing to report the incident, his not telling Adams, and—at first—his not telling Ina. To him, the key aspect is whether anyone was killed. His behavior suggests that only then would the event be worth thinking about.

There are indeed a number of questions about Ingham's behavior. For instance, why did Ingham not attempt to scare off the intruder by screaming or rushing to lock the door? Why did he not report the event to the hotel management, if not to the police? Last, there is another, more subtle, and peculiarly Highsmithian way in which the language suggests that the Arab's life is not valued particularly highly. Two minutes after the body has been dragged away, someone returns to wipe what Ingham knows to be blood off the tiles outside his bungalow. That person leaves while Ingham waits a moment:

Then he set his reading lamp on the floor, so its light would not show much through the shutters, and turned it on. He was interested in his typewriter.

The lower front part of the frame was bent. Ingham winced at the sight of it, more for the surprising appearance of the typewriter than for the impact it must have made against the head of the old Arab. Even the spacer had been pushed awry, and one end stuck up. A few keys had been bent and jammed together. Ingham flicked them down automatically, but they could not fall into place. The bend in the frame went in about three inches. That was a job for Tunis, all right, the repairing. (*Tremor*, 95)

Ingham's concern for the typewriter is a moment in the text where his own values, which privilege property over life—suggested earlier in the description of the typewriter falling "with a painful clatter" (*Tremor*, 94) and strikingly revealed in that the cause of his "wincing" is the damage done to a metal object in its contact with a human skull rather than the reverse—join those of the author. Highsmith's preoccupation with objects is so marked as to present a movement of the text on manifest and latent levels toward positively sanctioning the value of property over human life. In these descriptions, the attribution of sensation to the inorganic object and the implicit withdrawal of sensation from the human being is striking as Highsmith depicts the mechanism that allows one person to inflict violence on another by viewing him as less than human.

This issue is explored again, and at some length, in connection with the death of Jensen's dog, Hasso. The dog is disliked by the Arabs in the town of Hammamet, where Jensen lives in a building in the Arab quarter. (Ingham later moves into the apartment below him.) Early in the novel, the dog is missing, and Jensen assumes the Arabs have murdered him. " 'He's apt to tear them [strangers] apart,' Jensen said. 'He hates crooked Arabs, and he can tell them a mile off' " (*Tremor*, 77). " 'They'll toss his head in the door tomorrow morning,' Jensen said, 'or maybe his tail' " (*Tremor*, 78). The devaluation of the Arab is then made explicit when Jensen, listening to Ingham wonder whether he had killed the intruder, says, " 'I hope you got him. . . . That particular Arab was a swine. I like to think you got him, because it makes up a little for my dog—just a little. However, Abdullah wasn't worth my dog.' Ingham felt suddenly better. 'That's true' " (*Tremor*, 125). A passage such as this must give the reader pause. How are we meant to react? It is a safe assumption that few readers will endorse either character's utterances.

Although there is no problem with respect to Jensen, who is presented throughout as an embittered and, if you will, melancholy Dane, the case with respect to Ingham is quite different. Although it is not necessary that we identify positively with Ingham, still, as the novel's center of consciousness, he has to hold our interest, and to do this, his response to events, his actions or lack of actions, have to be of some importance. Yet there is an odd inconsequentiality to Ingham that, in different ways, critics have noted.[6] We are taken aback by Ingham's lack of response. He is really something of a moral vacuum, underlined in his realization that "he needed a great deal of reassurance" (*Tremor,* 125). Although superficially he comes with the normal charge of moral electricity, his batteries quickly run down. This is not true for any of the other three characters, who are all consistent and in little need of reassurance, whether it be Adams's naive American patriotism, Jensen's cynical European chauvinism, or Pallant's Protestant individualism. All are free of any conflict with respect to their values.

Ingham, however, is conflicted. He focuses obsessively on whether or not anyone has actually been killed. If this can unequivocally be proved to be the case, then he will *consider* informing the police, or at least the hotel management. Yet this is an odd technicality to focus on, as if one's moral code kicks in only once a certain threshold of damage has been reached. This moral vacillation underlines the labile quality of Ingham's personality and, most important, the novel's weltanschauung. Ingham says at one point that "Africa does turn things upside down" (*Tremor,* 136). One implication is that in the United States, Ingham would have acted differently, and twice reference is made to the fact that Abdullah's death is not President Kennedy's and that Arabs themselves do not value life as highly as do westerners. The temptation is strong to link this to the theme of the Vietnam War and the United States' role in that war. Although the link is never directly made between the two situations, the political discussions between Ingham and Adams indicate that the war is not far removed from the characters' consciousness. A kind of Hamiltonian view is suggested here, the idea that once entering the sphere of foreign relations, whether at the personal or the national political level, moral values lose their relevance.[7]

One minor example indicates a confusion at a more universal level than at the level of an individual character (where we might be more likely to attribute such confusion to authorial control). In the depiction of Adams's clandestine propaganda activity, it is suggested that he is being supported by an anti-Communist group within the Soviet Union.

However, his broadcasts are so naive and obviously propagandistic that they will rebound in the favor of the Soviet Union. Two things seem to reveal authorial confusion or conflict here. First, it simply is not plausible that such an organization could operate freely within the Soviet Union during that period, and second, it is also not plausible to think that no matter how unsophisticated the broadcasts, the Soviet or other Communist governments would ever fail to take the broadcasts seriously. The suggestion that either could occur betrays—behind a thin veneer of sophistication—a denial of the importance of politics generally. Ostensibly, Highsmith has always focused on the individual, and it is partially because of the complete omission of politics and the social as overt presences in the earlier novels that the presence of politics in *The Tremor of Forgery* is so striking. Yet the text's unstable political oscillations are reflected in both the labile quality of Ingham's emotions and the serious treatment of Adams's absurd political activity.

Moreover, Ingham's moral lability is counterpointed by a suggestion that his sexual identity is in question, a moment where Gide's *Immoralist* makes its presence felt. That novel dealt with a young European middle-class intellectual who comes with his wife to Algeria for his health. While there, he becomes aware of his homosexual desires and through this awareness of the importance of a break with European conventions. His stay in North Africa leads to a break with his wife and his previous way of life. For westerners, North Africa has long represented an attractive sexual freedom with men, women, and boys easily procurable. This can lead to a lowering of the barriers that are erected in Western cultures against what is viewed as deviant behavior. Highsmith clearly suggests the possibility of this occurring with Howard Ingham but, true to form, does not have him cross that line. Early in the novel, Jensen, who is homosexual, asks Ingham if he would like to have sex with him. Ingham refuses, appearing genuinely uninterested. Yet at other moments, he seems willing at least to consider the idea, and his reluctance is less than convincingly analyzed: "And Ingham recalled one night when he'd gone along to the coffee-house Les Arcades, and had come near to taking home a young Arab. The Arab had sat at the table with him, and Ingham had stood him a couple of beers. Ingham had been both sexually excited and lonely that evening, and the only thing that deterred him, he thought, was that he hadn't been sure what to do in bed with a boy, and he hadn't wanted to feel silly" (*Tremor,* 230). Ina later accuses Ingham of being interested in Jensen. And it is clear that socially, Ingham's relationship with Jensen interests him more than does his relationship with Ina. On the other hand, his sexual relationship with Ina is fine, as it was with his former wife. But—further muddying the waters—shortly after his arrival in Tunisia, he goes to bed with Katherine Darby, a young woman he has met on the beach, but he is impotent.

What are we to make of these various and sometimes contradictory indications? In the end, it does not seem that Highsmith has effectively established a situation analogous to that in Gide's novel. First of all, Ingham does not possess the psychological depth necessary to present such a psychic struggle convincingly, and furthermore the issue is a minor point in the novel. The question of whether Ingham should admit to having hurled the typewriter and possibly caused the death of the Arab is far more charged morally than the discussion of his sexual interests. The latter's function is rather to underline what we might characterize as the global indecision of Ingham's character.

Ingham's indecision and anxiety about his relationship with Ina and the text's ambivalent response to the politics of the era produce an interesting linguistic phenomenon related to what I have called "the flight into objects." The discussion of this aspect can best be introduced by recalling the moment when Ingham hurls his typewriter at the nocturnal intruder. I noted Ingham's feeling for the damage to the typewriter as well as the object's attainment of *sensation,* its ability to feel pain. This use of objects functions to control both a character's emotions and the movement of the text itself. A good example occurs in chapter 17. Ingham has gone to the Tunis airport to meet Ina Pallant. It is a crucial moment for Ingham because Ina has written him of her infidelity. Waiting in a restaurant where "there were some thirty white-clothed tables and a buffet-table of cold cuts near the big windows which gave on the airfield" (*Tremor,* 152), Ingham sees Ina "through a half-glass fence or wall." She is "in a loose white coat, white shoes, carrying a big colorful pocket-book and a sack which looked like two bottles of something" (*Tremor,* 152). After meeting her, his second question is "Where's your luggage? Let's get that settled" (*Tremor,* 153). A little later, "He watched her small, strong hands opening the pack of Pall Malls, lighting one with the strange-looking matchbook from New York, dark red with an Italian restaurant's name printed on it in black" (*Tremor,* 153). Shortly thereafter, they go for lunch to a restaurant in Tunis:

> He had never seen her like this. Surely part of it was the strain of the trip, he thought. "Don't try to talk about it. I can imagine—Try this Tunisian starter. Turns up on every menu."

> He meant the antipasto of tuna, olives, and tomatoes. Ingham had
> persuaded her to have scallopine, on the grounds that *couscous* was all too
> prevalent in Hammamet. (*Tremor,* 155)

Ingham executes the flight into things that is so conspicuous a feature of
Highsmith's texts. His anxiety is such that he cannot bring himself to
discuss important emotional issues brought on by Ina's infidelity. The
repressed tension pressures him to take refuge in the concrete reality of
things. And this concrete reality often displaces the feelings of Highsmith's characters.

Just as Ingham's initial impulse is to get the baggage "settled," that
is, under control, so the text's impulse is to settle things through occu-
pying itself with an inordinate amount of the prosaic baggage of
description. There seems to be a connection between this heightened
emphasis on detail and moments related to Ingham's anxiety about his
relationship with Ina. When he arrives to pick up Ina for dinner on the
night of her arrival, "[s]he was in a pink sleeveless dress with a big, cool-
looking green flower printed on the dress above one breast" (*Tremor,*
162). In such instances, Highsmith's use of detail—or rather its function in her work—goes well beyond the need to establish character or
setting. In fact, the use of detail ultimately works against those functions by overwhelming the text. The plethora of detail in such a sentence irresistibly shifts the text away from the person and toward the
object, which becomes the true subject of the sentence. Although such
prose may produce a strikingly flat surface, it is not a "degree zero" of
writing but rather a large negative number.[8] Rather than the detailed
description producing a thick depiction, in the manner of Balzac or
Zola, the greater the preponderance of the substantives, their adjectives,
and connectives, the more we are distanced from any reality beyond
these objects, which take on a life of their own and stand between the
characters and the reader. It is almost as if the characters possess an
exoskeleton of things that block entrance into their emotions.

The Tremor of Forgery executes an envoi to the existentialist moment
that significantly affected much of Highsmith's earlier work. Such issues
as choice, authenticity, and bad faith provide her novel with a significant
part of its thematic for the last time as they come under the pressure of
the explosive social issues of the 1960s. Hence, for both protagonist and
author, there are several powerful and sometimes conflicting dynamics
that have to be controlled. The ending, although unconvincing and
not particularly well motivated in novelistic terms—Ingham considers

returning to his ex-wife—is pressured by its historical context. Ingham cannot deal with the political and social changes represented and brought into his consciousness by the events of his stay in Tunisia; hence his renewed interest in Lotte, his ex-wife, represents an attempt to efface all that has occurred, to deny both his own and the world's history.

A Dog's Ransom (1972)

Three years after *The Tremor of Forgery,* Highsmith published *A Dog's Ransom,* a novel that more directly reflects its times than any other she ever wrote. Not coincidentally, it was also the first novel Highsmith set completely in New York City. A further anomaly is that it is High-smith's only novel to have a policeman as its protagonist, and this too results from the novel's attempt to come to terms with the socioeco-nomic changes of the 1960s. As a result, Clarence Duhamell, the police-man, is one of Highsmith's most contradictory and ambivalent cre-ations. Yet the contradictions and confusions spring not so much from her philosophical worldview (as in earlier novels) as from the novel's engagement with the social strains appearing in American society.

While Clarence Duhamell is Highsmith's first police protagonist, Kenneth Rowajinski, "the Pole," is the first proletarian to figure signifi-cantly in any of her novels, and this results from the novel's relation to the class conflicts of its historical period. The novel disguises the class nature of the conflict it describes, but it was not alone in doing this, as the conflicts of the 1960s manifested themselves culturally as well as politically, and at times the strands were entangled with one another, as they were in the antiwar movement. In the end, though, *A Dog's Ransom* reveals social and economic conflict more clearly than any of the author's other novels.[9] But at the same time, the author's inability to resolve suc-cessfully any of these conflicts makes *A Dog's Ransom* both an authentic expression of its times and an unusually moving, if flawed, novel.

Kenneth Rowajinski, a former construction worker now living on a disability pension, successfully extorts two separate payments of $1,000 each from Edward Reynolds, claiming to have dognapped Reynolds's poodle, Lisa, in Riverside Park one fall afternoon. (In reality Rowajinski killed Lisa with a stone immediately after she had strayed into some bushes as Reynolds walked her in the park.) A young policeman, Clarence Duhamell, more or less assigns himself to the case after Reynolds has notified the police of the ransom notes, as the police are otherwise too busy to devote it much attention. Duhamell soon discovers the perpetrator, but after being held in Bellevue for a while, Rowajinski is released. He then starts annoying Duhamell's girlfriend, Marilyn Coomes, who complains to Duhamell. One night Clarence finds Rowajinski near Marilyn's apartment in the Village, pursues him, and bludgeons him to death with his service revolver. Duhamell eventually admits his crime to Ed and Greta Reynolds (with whom he has become friendly) and to Marilyn, but denies it to the police, who, however, soon enough suspect him of the murder.

Clarence Duhamell's relationships with Ed and Greta Reynolds, with Marilyn, with the policemen Santini and Manzoni, and with Kenneth Rowajinski become the vehicle for an exploration of various social issues as Highsmith engages the changes wrought by the movement against the Vietnam War, by the youth counterculture (especially the movement for greater sexual freedom), and by the second wave of feminism (begun in the 1960s and coming into its own in the early 1970s). Highsmith, who had been living in Europe for a decade, confronts these issues at a remove through Duhamell's clumsy and awkward grappling with them.

Perhaps even more than in previous novels, there are a number of oddities about *A Dog's Ransom* that strike the reader: a notably unsuccessful attempt at colloquialisms, unrealistic plot events, and an unrealistic ending.[10] These failings are more significant because *A Dog's Ransom* is Highsmith's most sustained attempt at presenting the social totality, and thus aspects that we might view as relatively unimportant in studies focused on obsessed individuals assume greater prominence here. Undoubtedly the most striking oddity in *A Dog's Ransom,* and it is a masterful oddity, is that it is a *dog's* ransom. This fact trivializes the issue and, as a corollary, the Reynoldses and their concerns as well. It inevitably diminishes their importance as individuals by showing them as inextricably caught up in their own little world (and Lisa is not just a poodle; she is a miniature poodle). Indeed, lest we lose sight of the fact that the Reynoldses represent a class, both their friends and Ed's coworkers respond to the loss of Lisa in the same manner. Moreover, it is stated that the loss of the dog was as devastating for Ed as had been the earlier loss of his teenage daughter.

That middle-class stratum of technical-professional intellectuals with whom Highsmith's fiction had been so exclusively concerned has here been weakened in its presence and marginalized in importance. Ed Reynolds is at quite a remove from active technocrats such as David Kelsey or Robert Forester, or even a figure such as Howard Ingham in

The Tremor of Forgery, who attempt to control their destinies. Indeed, through the death of Ed's daughter from his first marriage and Ed and Greta's failure to have a child, this class is revealed as incapable of confronting the new historical and cultural forces in its most basic function, reproduction. Moreover, that it cannot even be left alone to its harmless and minor (Lisa, though pedigreed, is "from an inferior kennel") displays of conspicuous consumption does not bode well. In this respect, *A Dog's Ransom* marks something of a sea change in Highsmith's novels, prefigured by *A Tremor of Forgery*. If the earlier novel had explicitly indicated concerns with domestic unrest in the United States and doubts about America's role in the world, *A Dog's Ransom* leaves no doubt that in New York City, the central metropolis of the world's metropolitan center, the 1960s had transformed American society. My discussion focuses on three areas that clearly reflect these changes: social class, the sixties, and the function of Clarence Duhamell as the state's attempted mediator of the conflicts surrounding these issues.[11]

Social Class

A Dog's Ransom is Highsmith's first novel in which a distinctly proletarian figure plays an important, indeed crucial, role, and it should come as no surprise that Highsmith's first detailed depiction of the working class produces a somewhat atypical proletarian, one who has an independent income. Kenneth Rowajinski "had been a semi-skilled laborer in construction work, good at pipe-laying, a good foreman in the sense that some men are good army sergeants though they may never rise higher."[12] But Rowajinski has been injured four years before the novel begins, having lost one of the toes on his right foot in a job-related accident.[13] Although he receives a workers' compensation pension of $260 per month, he is an aggrieved and embittered man who has taken to writing anonymous letters, including two to the Reynoldses after he has killed their dog.

There are several odd elements in Highsmith's portrait of Rowajinski that suggest he is the locus of some unstated concerns. Although Rowajinski is the grandson of "a Polish immigrant who had come to America just before the First World War and married a German girl" (*Dog's,* 49), he is referred to dozens of times as "the Pole." Although his German descent might—on the basis of the information given—be just as easily emphasized, we can perhaps accept Highsmith's characterization because of his obvious Polish surname. But the key feature is not so much the standard procedure of hypo-descent as the fact that, though a second-generation American, Rowajinski is virtually denied citizenship through the constant reference to him as "the Pole."[14] In fact, ethnicity serves two functions in the novel. First, because ethnicity has become hypertrophied, even reified, it is not meant to refer to any material quality that might actually be related to ethnic origin. Other than the names themselves, there is little ethnically identifying about these characters. The constant use of the phrase "the Pole" to denominate this unsavory character, with nothing further than this literal conjunction, results in a kind of low-key racism. It seems to absolve the author of the need for much further characterization.

In fact, if we consider the moment of the novel's composition, it is clear that ethnicity is substituting for race. Ethnicity is meant to suggest the vaguely threatening Other, which, by the 1960s, as a result of the demands of the civil rights movement, had become incorporated for many middle-class white Americans in black Americans. Highsmith materializes the Other through ethnicity rather than race for two reasons. First, she would at all costs want to avoid anything suggestive of overt racism, and—although she was writing at a remove in Europe—the effect of increased African-American self-assertiveness would have made her aware of the dangers of stereotyping in this area.[15] Second, for someone of her class, who had lived in New York from the late 1920s through the 1950s, it was Southern and Eastern Europeans who constituted the most immediate "threat." Hence the backlash arising in reaction against African-American militancy (manifested, for example, in Saul Bellow's novel *Mr. Sammler's Planet* [1970] and shortly thereafter in Michael Winner's film *Death Wish* [1974]) would not have attracted Highsmith for a number of reasons. The overdetermined use of ethnicity is continued in the prominence of Italians among the police. That these two groups—Southern and Eastern Europeans—would seem to be Clarence's primary antagonists in 1970s New York City is remarkable. Clearly the social groups seen as most threatening at that time were blacks and Puerto Ricans. But Highsmith does not attempt the direct depiction of white *ressentiment* Bellow and Winner did.[16] Indeed, proof of the extent to which she avoids doing so is clear in her making the police predominantly Italian, rather than Irish, which would have been more faithful to both reality and its stereotyping. But the Irish had become so assimilated, especially in the large Eastern cities, that the element of difference and otherness that the threat must possess would be lacking.

A further intriguing aspect of Kenneth Rowajinski is that in spite of his clear proletarian provenance, Highsmith has once again detached the character from the realm of alienated labor by giving him an independent income, here in the form of his disability pension. Although Highsmith's protagonists often have—to varying degrees—independent sources of income, Rowajinski, along with Dickie Greenleaf and Vic Van Allen, has enough to live on. That Highsmith completely detached her one worker from work is revealing and especially so in the light of the shifts that *A Dog's Ransom* otherwise indicates. Yet in spite of the fact that Rowajinski is no longer constrained by the job, he is clearly a proletarian and represents that class as a threat, indicated not so much in his behavior as in the response it evokes.

The Reynoldses, on the other hand, are the most recent incarnation in that long line of middle-class couples that began with Guy Haines and Anne Faulkner and came to an end only with Jack and Natalia Sutherland in *Found in the Street,* a decade and a half later. Although the earlier couples had sometimes been threatened, the threat was always from an individual, always of their own class and in no way representative of anything beyond his own individual motives. Such is not the case in *A Dog's Ransom.* Although Kenneth Rowajinski is portrayed as mildly disturbed and a loner, it is within a social setting where the threats are many and varied, and I think this allows us to see him as representing something beyond himself. Moreover, Rowajinski's grievances possess an element of class resentment. In his second note to Ed Reynolds, Rowajinski writes

> Well Sir,
> Still at it? You are a little machine. You think the majority is with you. Not so! Since when are you so right? Just because you have a job and a wife and a snob dog like yourself? It need not go on forever till you creep into your grave. Think again and think carefully.
> Anon. (*Dog's,* 44)

It is not that Highsmith aimed at an analysis of social class in the United States but rather that her creation of Rowajinski as an important figure signals this political issue forcing its way into the novel.[17]

Closer to Highsmith's concerns is the troubled state of the American middle class, the most vivid manifestation of which is its inability to successfully reproduce itself or even to identify the "threat." Ed Reynolds had a daughter from his first marriage, Margaret, about whose death "he could not bring himself to think profoundly" (*Dog's,* 9). Her death is unusual: "[H]is promising daughter . . . had fallen in with a lot of young crumbs and died of drugs—no, rather she'd been shot in a brawl. Why had he thought of drugs? She'd been trying drugs, yes, that was true, but the drugs had not killed her. The shot had killed her. In a bar in Greenwich Village. The police had rounded up the boys with the guns, but it had been extremely vague just who fired that particular shot, and in a way it didn't matter to Ed" (*Dog's,* 10). That Ed Reynolds cannot identify the source of his daughter's death underlines the disorientation that is affecting middle-class life and its perception of the "threat" as both global and diffuse.

The state of the world being what it is, Ed and Greta have resolved not to have a child. While Greta Reynolds is depicted as unfailingly kind, sympathetic, and supportive of Ed, she is also portrayed as defeated by her trials as a Holocaust survivor. Indeed, she has been so shattered that she has given up her career as a concert pianist and stays home. As a result, all their emotions have been invested in Lisa, their miniature poodle. But here, too, we have something new in Highsmith. In previous novels, a dog would have had a great deal of commodified value. But now the fabric of value is beginning to fray a bit, as Lisa is "not the very best kennel, but still a pure poodle" (*Dog's,* 8). Most revealing is that it is several times stated that Ed's feelings for Lisa, or for her loss, equal those felt for the loss of his daughter. This transvaluation of values is shocking (though the novel does its best to naturalize it), which Ed seems to recognize but is powerless to alter: "A dog, a daughter—there should be a great difference, yet the feeling was much the same" (*Dog's,* 101). It is a sign of his complete defeat. Furthermore, in an indication that more is involved here than one individual's idiosyncratic reaction, Highsmith takes pains to show us that it is not just Ed who reacts so strongly to the loss of Lisa. Others respond just as strongly, and one of the novel's best scenes shows Ed and Frances, his secretary, telling how Lisa came to the office a number of times: " 'She'd make the rounds at a party, greet everybody, and people would give her canapés—' Frances broke off smiling. 'And she'd always sit up after she took anything, just as if she were saying thanks' " (*Dog's,* 142). The bathetic quality of the passage underlines the decline of the middle class, and it is revealing that Highsmith portrays it in such a light.

The Sixties

Looked at broadly, *A Dog's Ransom* is a response to the various social, political, and cultural changes that we have come to label "the sixties":

the youth counterculture (including the newfound freedom with respect to sex and drugs), the anti–Vietnam War movement, and women's liberation.[18] For the middle class, the sixties challenged its sociocultural hegemony, and the novel reflects this challenge in the fate of Ed Reynolds's daughter, Margaret, in (if not at) the hands of the counterculture and in the fate of Lisa, the Reynoldses' poodle, at the hands of Rowajinski. The retreat of the middle class is enacted in a striking scene of sterile domesticity when Greta prepares coffee for Ed, who is buried in an arcane and uninteresting biography of an obscure historical figure, which his firm is "probably going to publish." Greta prepares Ed's coffee, and "then he heard the cozy, intermittent hum of her sewing machine from the room that had been Margaret's" (*Dog's*, 32). Greta has been irrevocably damaged by history, and now Ed, through the loss of his daughter and then his dog, has suffered a similar fate. Greta's withdrawal into the most traditional feminine domesticity in effect denies the changes the women's movement was bringing into existence in women's lives, and the fact that it is the dead daughter's room underlines the regression at the personal level as well.

On the other hand, the novel depicts a more dynamic response to the sixties through Marilyn Coomes, Clarence's girlfriend, and in his attempt to come to terms with her demands. Marilyn is strident and opinionated and in the end something of a caricature: a figure that existed not so much in fact as in the overheated conservative imagination, threatened by the movements for social and sexual equality of that decade. Yet the novel reveals an ambivalence toward its creation. Although Marilyn is rigidly stereotyped as a countercultural figure—she wears a cape made from a Viet Cong flag, frequently refers to the police as "Fuzz" and "Pigs," and has a Castro poster on a wall of her apartment—she is also shown as responsible in her work as a freelance typist, not leaving her apartment for fear of missing phone calls for jobs and staying home at night working. She functions as a foil to Clarence, defining him more clearly. One good example of this occurs in reference to the student demonstrations of the sixties. Marilyn tells Clarence:

> "But we're not cut out for each other. We're too unlike. It's like you told me about Cornell—the student demonstrations."
>
> "Oh, that!" He was suddenly impatient. He had told Marilyn he had balked at wrecking the library and the faculty's offices, having gone along with the anti-war demonstrators, even made a speech or two at the rallies, up to that point, the point where they had talked of what Clarence still

> remembered he had called "perfectly innocent, perfectly good and even beautiful books—and furniture!" Marilyn had turned against him because of this: she professed to see a reason why "everything old" had to be destroyed before something new and better could be built. (*Dog's,* 151)

This passage reveals specific political positions of *A Dog's Ransom,* the irruption of the political as such into Highsmith's novels, and a strange charm resulting from the conflict between manifest and latent political content.

Marilyn is depicted as extreme, even irrational, Clarence as reasonable. But Marilyn is shown through Clarence's unsympathetic eyes; though "she professed to see a reason," the reader is not allowed to hear the reason, censored as it is by Clarence. Moreover, there is no context for the demonstration, other than the vague reference to Cornell. It is presented almost ahistorically, and this suggests that the novel is not attempting to explore the meaning of specific events so much as reacting to them. Not unexpectedly, it betrays more than a little confusion in Clarence's stance vis-à-vis these events. The syntax emphasizes Clarence's balking and plays down his "going along," though he had "made a speech or two" at the rally. In other words, he has not "gone along." Yet it is unclear exactly what he did; there is only the vaguest clue as to what his speeches were about, that is, he did not want property—"innocent books and furniture"—destroyed. The vagueness robs his stance of any political content.[19] Indeed, with the somewhat odd qualifier "innocent," we have an example of that peculiar Highsmithian relationship to objects that is one of the intriguing aspects of these novels, reminiscent of Ingham's injured typewriter. It is, in short, the attribution of affective, moral qualities to material objects, the attribution of the spiritual to the material, which, though becoming less prominent as her career progresses, remains a presence.

The confusion evident in the novel's response to the Vietnam War is also apparent in its treatment of sexuality. Although the increase in sexual freedom was one of the dominant and irrevocable—though contested—achievements of the sixties, the response of *A Dog's Ransom* is an anxious ambivalence. On the one hand, much is made of the fact that, though unmarried, Clarence spends nights at Marilyn's apartment (to which he possesses the keys). Yet such nights notwithstanding, even at the level of intimate sexual relations, sexuality is constrained and, in a sense, absent from the novel. This is apparent in the most intimate scene in the novel. Clarence has gone to the Village to visit Marilyn, stopping at a delicatessen on the way, and Marilyn is still in bed when he arrives:

> Marilyn was in bed with the papers, looking beautiful, though she hadn't even combed her hair. "How was it?"
> Clarence knelt by the bed, the delicatessen bag on the floor. "Interesting," he mumbled. His face was buried in the warm sheets over her bosom. He inhaled deeply. "Very interesting. It's important." (*Dog's*, 45)

The fussy detail of the delicatessen bag on the floor produces an almost humorous effect, distancing the reader; indeed, one senses a constraint that will not allow Clarence's body to touch Marilyn's directly. But the novel's anxiety vis-à-vis the sexual is also revealed not so much through Clarence as through his employer, the police. At moments it is suggested that his sleeping over at his girlfriend's may be a mark against him in the department. It is hard to imagine that this was ever an issue for urban policemen at any point after World War I; in any event, it is wildly anachronistic for the early 1970s in New York and underlines the novel's problem in grappling with the issue.

The question of sexuality should also be seen in relation to a larger topic, feminism. Because feminism is viewed in the novel as part of the broader, more global "threat" of the changes produced in the 1960s, the role of women is presented more conservatively in *A Dog's Ransom* than it had been in the novels of the preceding decade, such as *The Glass Cell* and *The Tremor of Forgery*. This is clear in the area women's liberation saw as of supreme importance, work. Greta Reynolds, for example, has withdrawn from the labor force, and women otherwise appear in subordinate roles as office workers. Marilyn herself has quit college and works as a freelance secretary. She is, however, an ambiguous creation, her independence manifesting itself in the political and cultural sphere. Although something of a caricature, she does have a mind of her own. The third female presence in the novel, Ed's daughter, Margaret, has been killed before the novel begins. But it is she, a woman, who dies at the hands of the sixties. Although the circumstances of her death are vague, she has used drugs (a prime marker for "the sixties"), and she has been killed. This, we seem to hear the novel saying, is what happens to women who assert their independence.

The Police and the Ending

Although *A Dog's Ransom* is of average length for a Highsmith novel (usually around 250 pages), it seems longer. The impression of length derives from the extended conflict between Clarence and the police, most notably the repeated interrogations he undergoes at their hands and the interrogations' reverberations on the other characters. The length of this section reflects the novel's inability to come to terms with the conflicts it is depicting and a shift in emphasis. Throughout the first third, there is the possibility that Kenneth Rowajinski might well be the novel's antagonist. Yet he is killed relatively early, and it might be that Highsmith's intentions shifted in the course of composition, and attention was shifted to Clarence. What started out as a conflict between Clarence and the proletarian Rowajinski is transformed, after Clarence murders Rowajinski, into a conflict between Clarence and the police. This displaces the original problematic from a class conflict to a conflict within the mediating force of the state.

The role of the police, a role much greater than in any previous novel, reflects the decline of the middle class in that it can no longer resolve conflicts on its own, as for example by hiring private detectives *(Strangers on a Train)* or by its own members *(Deep Water)*. That the central figure of the novel is a policeman—the only time this occurs in any of Highsmith's novels—underlines the fact that the novel's conflict is societal and as such cannot be resolved privately.[20] The constellation of forces threatening the established order is so great that the previous individualistic solutions no longer obtain. The importance of the police is a sign as well that the conflicts have gone beyond the realm of individual interest; they are neither within nor between individuals so much as they are social. Yet such a problematic—the threatened middle class, the threatening Other (i.e., the proletariat cum counterculture)—cannot be resolved by the state. This dilemma and its failed displacement onto the state contribute to the elongated denouement.

Because the structure of social relations, in toto, is at stake, a more drastic resolution had to be attempted. Hence the increased role the state plays as the police, and most poignantly Clarence, try to suture the tear in the social fabric. Yet the inherent weakness of the attempt is shown through the conflict between Clarence and the detectives Manzoni and Santini,[21] a conflict whose troubled nature is manifested both in the particular lack of realism in the portrayal of the police and in Clarence's ultimate death at their hands. First of all, it strains credulity that the police would behave as brutally toward one of their own as they do toward Clarence, who undergoes a minor third-degree procedure. (Indeed, what we know of the police suggests the opposite: they often spend a good deal of their energies protecting their own.) Police brutality is suffered by racial minorities and the poor (and, of course, it is

Rowajinski who has been manhandled and then killed by a policeman), and to present it as Highsmith does here, directed against one of their own (and a white, Ivy League graduate to boot), is further evidence of the novel's difficulty coming to terms with contemporary social conflicts. Yet Clarence's victimization by the police and by the novelist is understandable given Highsmith's worldview. Inclined to see things only from the individual perspective, she is constrained in any social analysis to the individual. Responding to changes that were social in nature, she was at a loss as to how to have her idiosyncratic protagonists become representative. Clarence Duhamell, though sane and unexceptional, is far too unrepresentative a figure to effect any satisfying resolution.

In the end, the detective Manzoni shoots Clarence, and though the ending is vague, it seems clear that Clarence dies, thinking as he does, "*I had wished for so much better*" (*Dog's*, 256). Indeed, an unusual amount of the novel is couched in the optative mood, revealing its idealism and suggesting the underlying ambivalence and confusion. From all the aspects discussed—class, feminism, sexuality, the Vietnam War, the counterculture, and the role of the state—the principal conclusion to be drawn is that the novel is unable to stake out a coherent position. Moreover, it is less the confusion, ambivalence, and irresolution of particular individuals present in previous novels (though that confusion may have had social roots to it) as it is a global and social confusion, in one sense an objective confusion. The 1960s was not an easy moment to come to terms with, and indeed is still very much with us, as the virulence of the current backlash to it makes clear.

Clarence's killing of Rowajinski, the act by which he attempts to suture together the torn relations between social classes through the power of the state, brings him down. This failure has to be seen in the end as a social failure. Whereas in novels such as *The Talented Mr. Ripley, Deep Water, Ripley Underground,* and *The Glass Cell,* the protagonists (though they were all criminals, murdering from personal motives and often pecuniary ones at that) survive, here the murderer is a policeman who murders out of "social" motives and is himself killed by the police. In the end, Clarence is punished. This is markedly at variance with how murderers usually fare in Highsmith's novels and results from the social nature of Clarence's retributive action. This attempt to take the law into one's own hands (though Clarence is a representative of the law) is negatively sanctioned, and the novel's suggestion as to why this should be so is intriguing. Clarence has stepped out of the private world that

Highsmith's characters hitherto occupied, in which they might do as they please. His death suggests that once out of the world of pure, undisguised self-interest, things become confusing. Although individuals such as Tom Ripley, Sydney Bartleby, and Howard Ingham are immoral, they are in one sense "harmless," in that theirs is a purely personal immorality, an "apolitical immorality," if you will. *A Dog's Ransom* suggests that when a character acts from altruistic motives, we have a real danger to society.

Edith's Diary (1977)

Edith's Diary is Highsmith's most ambitious novel. Concerns present in her novels over the previous two decades here culminate in an unusual kind of gesellschaftsroman. Although the themes of madness, of fantasy versus reality, and of the family were present in her earliest work, and politics and history began to surface in *The Tremor of Forgery* (1969) and *A Dog's Ransom* (1972), in *Edith's Diary,* two other interrelated issues assume prominence: the status of women and that most material aspect of human existence, the reproduction of life. Although one can only speculate on what lay behind Highsmith's decision to focus on these issues, the increasing force of the women's movement (for which Betty Friedan's 1963 book *The Feminine Mystique* is sometimes cited as a starting point) certainly played a part.[22]

The plot of *Edith's Diary* is one of Highsmith's simplest. Edith and Brett Howland (respectively a freelance writer and a journalist) and their child, Cliffie, move from Greenwich Village to Brunswick Corner, a small town in eastern Pennsylvania. Among other things, they contemplate starting a local newspaper. In the meantime, Brett works for the New York *Herald Tribune.* One result of their move from an apartment to a house is their taking in George Howland, Brett's 73-year-old uncle, a retired lawyer, to live with them. In the years following the move, Brett falls in love with Carol Junkin, a younger woman, and he and Edith divorce. For her part, Edith becomes more involved with the newspaper, the *Bugle,* while also taking a part-time job at a local gift shop, The Thatchery. Cliffie, on the other hand, does not attend college and lives at home, holding part-time jobs into his late twenties. Over time, George Howland becomes an increasing burden (finally becoming bedridden) to Edith, who dutifully continues to care for him long after Brett has left the household. Toward the end of the novel, Cliffie administers an overdose of codeine to George, which proves fatal. This marks the beginning of Edith's decline, and her accidental death comes as she resists the efforts of Brett and Gert Johnson (a friend with whom she runs the *Bugle*) to convince her to accept psychiatric help. As may be clear from this summary, this is Highsmith's least dramatic novel. It might also be noted that the novel covers 20 years, by far the longest time span of any of the novels. Yet for these reasons it becomes one of her most interesting character studies and perhaps her most engaged novel. Moreover, through its detailed description of Edith's daily existence, the reproduction of her life, the detailed representation of those "simple" tasks that we all have to accomplish in order to continue our existence, the novel presents a picture of life striking for its emphasis on the material aspects of human existence. In fact, its unusual treatment of material existence constitutes the novel's primary significance; its treatment of politics and its representation of sanity, madness, and the family are also important themes, and the latter in part derives from the main theme.

Housework, Reproduction of Life, and the Body

For a reader familiar with Highsmith's novels, the most unusual aspect of *Edith's Diary* is the amount of attention given to the aspects of daily existence that are basic to our continuing to reproduce our lives, the necessary tasks that allow us to engage in all the higher activities that, especially if we are middle class, we like to think of as our main concern. These necessary tasks involve making sure that we have food, shelter, and clothing, but even more specifically, *Edith's Diary* involves itself with such tasks as cleaning, preparing meals, transportation, and the like. In most fiction, these things are taken for granted, as they were in Highsmith's earlier novels.[23] All this has changed in *Edith's Diary*. Here they become something like the theme of the novel. As Edith remarks to herself, apropos of her having to care for George: "Edith couldn't imagine a man thirty-five or so not getting married, if he could afford to, because it was so convenient to have a wife, they performed so many services."[24] Indeed, Highsmith herself remarked of Edith that "her profession as housewife slowly and dreadfully kills her" (Loriot, 44).

This emphasis on the day-to-day material tasks of life is matched by the presence, in a way not previously encountered, of another material element, money. The protagonists of the earlier novels had been middle-class professional men who always possessed skills that could land them comfortable positions; they sometimes had independent incomes as well. (Indeed, it was not until the novels of the 1960s and 1970s that women working became something of a fixture in Highsmith's novels, though never the protagonists.) This is not the case with Edith. Although she is a Bryn Mawr graduate, she has never had much of a connection to the labor force. Finally forced into it by her divorce, she is positioned squarely in the "postindustrial" working class as a salesperson. Hence, unlike any previous Highsmith protagonist, Edith has problems making ends meet: "But after the electricity, oil for the heating and hot water, gas, and the telephone bill (lots of the telephone bill had to do with the *Bugle*), the car upkeep . . . and the house mortgage which would, thank God, be finished in another two years, and the crazy unexpecteds like the rusted boiler that had to be replaced a few months ago, there was nothing left at the end of the month, or Edith had to dip into the checking account at the Brunswick First National" (*Diary,* 117). This emphasis—indeed thematizing—of the problems of daily existence is not only new in itself but crucial in constructing the novel's feminist position. With the possible exception of *The Price of Salt, Edith's Diary* is Highsmith's most feminist novel. Whether it is a feminist novel will be discussed later.

Highsmith, when asked whether she ever wanted to create a "strong, active female character," responded, "Yeah, in a way, Edith. She was energetic. You could call her a housewife, ok, but she wrote" (Berch, 12).[25] But although Edith's journalistic activity is symbolically important, it does not amount to much, and she does not support herself by it. What focuses the novel and concretizes for us the image of Edith as active is exactly her activity as a housewife. In a backhanded way, this is acknowledged by Highsmith herself. When pressed to respond to one interviewer's assertion that "when she goes into her fantasy life, it's only a passive response to an impossible structural situation," Highsmith replied, "Yes, I know what you mean, because she didn't quit the house. She loved the house, the garden. . . . What she could have done was *quit* the house. . . . Look, men can leave the house. Ripley leaves his house. I don't see women leaving the house. . . . Edith leave the house? What the hell, where's she going? She can't do anything except be a shop seller" (Berch, 12–13). In reality, Edith could have "quit the house," but in truth the house gives her a sense of identity because in the house, her activity is materialized. For the wife, as Beauvoir wrote, "the home becomes the center of the world and even its only reality; 'a kind of counter-universe in opposition' (Bachelard): refuge, retreat, grotto, womb, it gives shelter from outside dangers; it is this confused outer world that becomes unreal."[26]

There almost always come moments in Highsmith's novels when we question the rationality of a character's behavior, and although there is nothing in *Edith's Diary* approaching Melinda Van Allen's perversely continuing to live with a man she believes to be a double murderer (in *Deep Water*), it is fair to wonder why Edith does not rid herself of Cliffie and George, the two burdens that prevent her from materially improving her existence. Questioned about Edith's inability to throw Cliffie out, Highsmith begged the question: "She just couldn't bring herself to do it" (Berch, 13). It is one instance of the remarkable passivity Highsmith's women characters sometimes reveal. But questions as to rationality are here less relevant than in the earlier novels because the character's situation is quite believable. In *Edith's Diary,* Highsmith powerfully depicts the role of women in the social division of labor. Hence Edith represents woman's function as providing material (and nonmaterial) support for men. Indeed, the uselessness of George and Cliffie makes all the more vivid Edith's position, which might otherwise be seen as productive (though unpaid) because it enabled a man's productivity (the typical housewife situation). It comes as no surprise, however, for Highsmith to depoliticize Edith's situation by removing the family constellation from the economy through George and Cliffie's unproductive behavior. Were it to be seen as political, there might also be seen a beginning to its end.

But materialism exists in a yet more basic and, for Highsmith (normally reserved about such things), somewhat shocking manifestation: that is, in the materiality of the body and its functions, and even more specifically with a disgust of the body and its functions. Eliminatory bodily functions are regarded with varying degrees of disgust. Hence the quasi fixation on these unpleasant aspects of the body through George Howland (who becomes increasingly unable to attend to his own basic needs) is remarkable. George Howland's only function in the novel is as an added burden to Edith of an especially repellent nature. The nature of the repulsion is suggested when Edith is shown as feeling relieved that George, at first, can manage his own bodily functions. But as he becomes increasingly helpless, the materiality of the imposition bulks larger till Edith balks at "the awful reality . . . the bedpans, the filthy handkerchiefs" (*Diary,* 137). The culmination of this burdensome presence takes place shortly before Cliffie administers the codeine overdose and directly results from his having left George unattended for not quite 24 hours while Edith is away attending her aunt Melanie's funeral. On Edith's return, she goes upstairs toward George's room:

Then she noticed the smell.

She knew, and without a pause plunged in. It was the carpets, the hall floor and *their* scatter rugs. Edith opened George's window, and continued to work with a will, with bucket, sponges, liquid rug cleaner. George was asleep through it all, snoring gently, despite the bumps of the plastic bucket as Edith set it out again and again. Next came the bedsheets. No, first the bedpan, just for a moment's relief, because it was so much easier to clean than what she had been cleaning. Even so, she had to leave it to soak in the bath-tub in five inches of water. Amazing! In not quite twenty-four hours! (*Diary,* 185)

Here Edith is portrayed as both submissive and active. "Without a pause," as if drawing from some well of womanly instinct, she knows what she has to do and does it. At the same time, there is no thought of rebelling or even of getting help from Cliffie, who caused the mess by leaving George unattended for so long.

Edith has become a "professional" care provider. But this entire transformation, of which this passage is the most vivid representation, has to be carefully examined and placed in a larger context within the novel and within the context of the women's movement in the 1970s. Edith is indeed active in the most literal physical sense, expending a good deal of physical energy, and, in a more general "administrative" sense, providing for George and Cliffie and, of course, herself as well. Yet looked at more broadly, she remains passive, refusing, for example, to rebuke Cliffie for leaving George unattended: she "was not going to mention it, because it would only give Cliffie satisfaction if she did" (*Diary,* 185). She cannot mobilize herself to prevail upon George to enter a nursing home, which he can afford, and Cliffie to leave home. Hence, we have Highsmith writing a novel in the mid-1970s—a peak moment of the contemporary women's movement (before the backlash of the 1980s)—which has a setting where the woman is preternaturally oppressed far beyond what was typical for women, especially women of Edith's middle-class provenance. In other words, did Highsmith, in trying to show women's housework burden, exaggerate to such an extent that Edith's extreme situation undermines a condition that would otherwise be unproblematically recognized as oppressing women? Although most elder and child care is done by women, Edith's situation seems extreme. It is odd that in none of the political articles Edith writes for the *Bugle* does she discuss the issue of women's economic exploitation, although it is something she has firsthand knowledge of. Seen from this perspective, Highsmith's presentation of Edith's oppression seems an attempt to naturalize it. Although Edith's oppression is clearly material, no alternative is even sketched; there is no escape other than death.

Cliffie, Edith's son, represents a second material intrusion of the body into the novel, and his character is the locus of several concerns. First of all, the depiction of Edith and Cliffie's relationship is the most detailed depiction of a parent-child relationship in Highsmith's fiction; Cliffie also becomes the vehicle for another distorted depiction of the liberated sexuality of the sixties; and last, Cliffie represents something like a proletarianized descendent of the Tom Ripley of *The Talented Mr. Ripley,* sans Ripley's insouciant amorality. Cliffie is a character who has no redeeming virtues. Indeed, we are introduced to him as he is trying to suffocate the family cat (foreshadowing his killing of George). Cliffie's complete reprobacy makes Edith's unwillingness to cut him loose all the more inexplicable.

Cliffie reminds us of Tom Ripley, too, in his self-centered quality, his self-indulgence, yet he is without the naked charm of Ripley's unconcealed consumerist desires—quite the opposite, indeed, as Cliffie functions as a perverted 1960s hippyist intrusion into the novel, willing to take the rewards of society's generalized increase in productivity in "released time," rather than material goods. Cliffie's life consists of an assortment of antisocial acts (theft, cheating, a suicide attempt, murder) and a series of part-time jobs. Last, there is a sense in which Cliffie is also a throwback to David Kelsey in *This Sweet Sickness,* as Cliffie fantasizes a relationship with a woman out of, one might say (in this instance, quite appropriately), whole cloth.

Cliffie's sexuality is the most striking aspect of his presence in the novel and at the same time his most materialized. It consists of masturbating into a sock: "Now as to girls, Cliffie thought, feeling philosophical as he began on his double rum, he took the attitude that it was safer for the time being to hold himself aloof. He could always jerk himself off and did if he felt so inclined. No complications there. He used his sock to come in, which caused him to wash them rather often, which earned him a word of praise from his mother!" (*Diary,* 79). Beyond the fact that the presence of a passage treating a topic as private and sexual as masturbation is unusual in Highsmith's fiction, there is a revealing detail. The use of the phrase "jerk himself off," rather than the less-marked "jerk off," emphasizes the alienated, split quality of Cliffie, even with respect to this most solipsistic of sexual acts. On the one hand, the appearance of actual sexual activity (and reference to Cliffie's masturbating occurs a number of times) represents a change from earlier novels.

But it also cannot be denied that the overall impression is one of strong distaste, if not disgust, for the topic. Yet Highsmith also obtains a reader response comprising sadness, discomfort, embarrassment, pathos, and, in the end, a feeling of alienation unlike anything experienced in more conventional authors, and this is no small achievement.

The masturbation scene occurs later in the novel, after Cliffie has had his first and only date with Lucy Beckman, a young woman from the Main Line. He never sees her again but continues to feel involved with her for several years, asking people in town if they have seen or heard of her and even placing a personals ad for three days running asking her to contact him. In the manner of David Kelsey (with respect to Annabelle Stanton) in *This Sweet Sickness*, Cliffie develops an active fantasy life around Lucy. But going one step further than David, Cliffie attempts, in her absence, to materialize her: "It had occurred to Cliffie to make a dummy of Luce for his room. He wouldn't necessarily sleep with it of course, but what a pleasure it would be to be able to see a life-sized figure of her, pretty and slim in her dark blue slacks, pink shirt—all made of what? Straw stitched into canvas, he supposed. The problem of the materials threw him off" (*Diary,* 251). What is odd indeed about this passage is that it represents a twofold materialization (literally) of the fantasy. First there is the dummy, but then, as if that is still too close to a living substance, Cliffie proceeds *not* to sleep with it but to objectify an already inorganic object in terms of its parts: slacks and shirt. The fear of intimacy—not sleeping with a dummy (!)—and the pleasure in the passive viewing (embodying control) resume, at an even more distanced level than usual, the problematic sexuality of the Highsmithian character, that is, the desire for intimacy and the reluctance to relinquish the control necessary for it.

An especially poignant moment in Cliffie's "relationship" with Lucy occurs after his one date. She had "said goodnight to him at the curb in front of his house. She hadn't wanted to come in" (*Diary,* 238). Cliffie is upset because he has failed to get her address: "He was a bit too pissed to torture himself further about this, so he washed and brushed his teeth in the kitchen, then fell into bed too tired to play with a sock, though in a moment of glory earlier in the evening, he had thought of that" (*Diary,* 239). This perfectly represents the odd pathos that Highsmith is a master at evoking: "glory" is the *thought* of *masturbating.* Highsmith's unusual talent lies in concretizing just these peculiar moments of the psyche in unexpected ways, precious in both senses of the word. She is expert at representing the smallest quiver of her characters' desires.

Another instance of Cliffie's masturbation manqué demonstrates this. Early in the novel, Cliffie hears of Brett's new secretary, Carol (whom Brett eventually marries). "His father had mentioned her nearly a month ago, a blonde Cliffie recalled his father saying, surely in her early twenties. . . . Cliffie went to bed again and tried to make it with the imaginary Carol, failed, and felt quite tired suddenly" (*Diary,* 82–83). Although Cliffie's oedipal sexuality is pathetic and clichéd, it is at the same time (and perhaps for the same reasons) strangely moving. Highsmith is able to concretize, no matter how "clumsily" (I use the quotation marks because the apparent clumsiness contributes to the effect), those small psychic quirks that we possess or that possess us—minor weirdnesses that hold a surprising power to disturb us. Highsmith has a talent for depicting, almost by refraction, these odd psychic interstices that are not particularly demeaning but before which we still feel a certain embarrassment. They are the odd little places invested by the libido or overmanaged by the superego. The experience of reading Highsmith's novels is like rummaging through a drawer or a closet in another person's presence and coming upon forgotten things that—for whatever reason—embarrass us: seventies bell-bottoms that we forgot we ever bought, let alone wore. We are embarrassed that we ever bought the stuff; why is it still here? Highsmith identifies a humanity manifested in oddly embarrassing libidinal investments.

Politics and the Political

Politically, *Edith's Diary* is Highsmith's most fascinating novel. In it the events of the 1960s and 1970s—the civil rights movement, Vietnam, and Watergate—threaten the carefully (one might say anxiously) preserved individualist ethos of the earlier novels and its political corollary, the formal democracy of the American political system. But the novel can mobilize no other political analysis as a fallback to clarify the historical events that threatened the efficacy of traditional American ideology. The results are Edith's confused, confusing, and contradictory views, which almost inevitably influenced perceptions of the novel's politics. Indeed, one reviewer felt that the novel's attempt to depict contemporary history flawed it.[27] On one level, this assessment is correct. Here, as elsewhere when Highsmith attempts to represent history, we are ultimately left with the feeling that the representation lacks authenticity, that it "only *names* political events . . . paints a sort of political border to this essentially private story" (Wood, 32). Yet, with the exception of *The Price of Salt*, Highsmith has never been a realist, certainly not in any naively referential sense. Her mimesis lies elsewhere, often more affecting and gaining force from the circumlocutious manner of its expression. Her novels remain private only if we do not analyze the politics of that privacy.

The novel's ambivalent stance toward American democracy appears on the first page of the second chapter. Edith has Thomas Paine's famous lines framed on her wall: ". . . These are the times that try men's souls. The summer soldier and the sunshine patriot will in this crisis shrink from the service of his country; but he that stands it NOW, deserves the thanks of man and woman. Tyranny, like hell, is not easily conquered. *The Crisis*" (*Diary*, 17, ellipsis in original). The Enlightenment rationalist Paine believed that an individual, through the use of reason, could affect the politics of his or her time, a belief in the transparency of language that the actual effect of Highsmith's novel and Edith's madness undermines. Following this quotation, we have a different perception of American democracy: "She had told Cliffie about Tom Paine, the English-born corset-maker who became a journalist, whose words had rallied the not always enthusiastic volunteer soldiers of Washington's army—which had brought their nation into being. She and Brett had taken Cliffie to see the cracked Liberty Bell in Philadelphia, and had in general tried to introduce him to his new Home State, which also included the battlefield of Gettysburg" (*Diary*, 17). Hence, even at, or before, its origin ("not always enthusiastic"), this symbolically ("cracked") and historically ("Gettysburg") divided nation is depicted as politically problematic.

But a discussion of the role Edith's political views play must consider several aspects. First, there is the issue of historical time (the time of the novel runs from the mid-1950s through the mid-1970s) and the time of the novel's composition. Next, there is the change in Edith's views from liberal to libertarian conservative. Last, there is the issue of her apparent increasing mental instability and thus the question of how we are to treat her increasingly conservative views in light of her psychological condition. In the end, however, Edith's views are only a part of the novel's politics; what is primary is an appreciation of what the novel as a whole suggests politically as well as how we are to read it in the context of *The Tremor of Forgery* (1969) and *A Dog's Ransom* (1972).

The first extended exposition of Edith's views comes in the form of a diary entry:

> 7/Nov./54. In New York people say politics don't interest them. "What can I do about it anyway?" This is the attitude government powers in America want to foster and do. News is brief, filtered and slanted. The Guatemalan "uprising" would have been far more interesting if social conditions there had been described and if United Fruit Company's activities had been exposed—by radio and TV. Discussion clubs should be set up all over America to talk about forces *behind* things. We have been brainwashed for decades (since 1917) to hate Communism. *Readers Digest* has never failed to print one article per issue about the inefficiency of anything socialized, such as medicine. (*Diary,* 19)

The tenor of the entry suggests someone in the 1950s with leftist political sympathies. Yet the language is odd. Why, for example, is "uprising" placed in quotation marks? And what is the effect of the use of "interesting" here? The entry suggests that politics has to be sold to the American public as something they would like if they just gave it a chance—like classical music, perhaps—rather than being something that concretely affects their lives. Last, the one specific measure advocated is the formation of discussion groups, but there is no suggestion that anything beyond talking is necessary. Later Edith works on an article on the advantages of socialized medicine, marking her as a domestic liberal, and throughout the novel, she opposes the Vietnam War. The problem with the representation of these views is that Highsmith gives us only slogans, at times close to clichés. There are no specific social, political, or economic events to which these slogans are attached. There is a hollow quality to Edith's politics, a general *bien-pensant* liberalism, lacking any originality or personal imprint. Part of the problem is that Highsmith is projecting back 10 and 20 years with little effort to root these dicta historically beyond the odd temporal markers: Eisenhower, Senator Sanders from Vermont, and Guatemala.

There are, however, other moments when Edith's politics are both more bizarre and more authentic. Edith presents Gert, coeditor of the *Bugle,* with a draft of an editorial related to the Peace Corps, "an editorial which never got printed . . . because it was too far out, or unrealistic":

> The American Peace Corps might take with them children aged eight to ten, since children of this age mix so well with children in any country, have no racial prejudice (at least not entrenched), and pick up languages quickly. Orphanages could be solicited for willing recruits, and perhaps there would be many. The Peace Corps activities involve camping and

adventure. Seeds of friendship would be planted, memories formed that
will not die even at the death of those who have them, because they will
pass them on to others. Lonely children, the abandoned, the illegitimate,
the discouraged, will find a place in society, and instead of being pitied,
they will become the heroes, the young pioneers, if they can be adopted
as junior members of the Peace Corps. (*Diary,* 94–95)

This passage comes well after Edith has begun distorting reality in her
diary, but before her entry into insanity (if she becomes insane). How
are we to construe such a passage? On the one hand, there is a poignant
sympathy and identification with the oppressed, yet these very same
oppressed are being tossed out of the country in a macabre manner. The
writer assumes that lonely, illegitimate, and abandoned children cannot
be helped in their native country. There is also a particularly revealing
idealist moment in that memories are viewed as capable of being passed
on from those who have the experience, and thus the memory of it, to
those who have not had it. This tenuous concatenation—experience,
memory of experience, experience of memory, and finally memory of
experience of memory—indicates the pure idealization of history that
underlies much of Highsmith's oeuvre. (How can you have a memory of
someone else's memory?) The passage unsettles the reader. Because we
do not know whether to take it seriously and because we do not know
whether it is connected to Edith's increasing emotional problems, it
becomes so disorienting that it brackets the entire question of the political as, indeed, undecidable.

Edith's views begin to shift as she slides into madness. Toward the
end of the novel, in a discussion with her friends Gert and Norm, she
herself finds her views shifting to the right, to a more authoritarian
position:

"There *is* one way to break this damned backwardness of the blacks," and
she put backwardness in quotes by the tone of her voice, "that's to take
them away from their parents when they're two or even one year old, and
bring them up among middle-class whites—you know with books and
music in the house and a stable home life. Then we'd see—"
 "Wha-at? Pretty drastic," Gert said, now bringing a big blue bowl of
peach ice cream to the table.
 "Yes," Edith went on in a gentle voice, thinking a soft approach might
sink in better, "but that's the only way to break the vicious circle. No
matter how good schools are, kids still spend more time out of school
than in. If colored kids were brought up in white households, we'd see—

or prove—that environmental and economic conditions are more important than heredity."

"Hear, hear!" said Norm.

Dinah had come in for the ice cream.

Edith wondered, however, if she really believed that environment was
more important than heredity. Over the ice cream, she found herself
reversing what she had said. She thought heredity was more important,
had a slight edge on environment, and she said so. Then Gert got up in
arms. This was racism.

"Aryan crap!" Gert said.

But Edith didn't back down. Lincoln learned his sums by writing on
the back of a shovel. Nobody had been pouring money into his schools.
(*Diary,* 245)

Not only the content of Edith's views but their labile quality undermine
them almost as she speaks. Whereas I think Highsmith wants us to see
the ease with which Edith takes up contradictory positions as a reflection of her increasingly unstable psychological state, there is—again—
also a level on which the reader cannot help but reflect on the meaninglessness of political positions generally, because there is just as much
reason for Edith to hold her conservative views as there had been for her
to hold her liberal views, that is, very little.

In the end, the formally political aspect of *Edith's Diary* is problematic. At one level, the clearest indication of the novel's politics is the
choice of a somewhat eccentric protagonist who, in the course of the
novel, becomes increasingly disturbed as the author's vehicle for a political statement. By making Edith lose her sanity, Highsmith invalidates
all of Edith's opinions, even, to a certain extent, those she held before
becoming mad because we have a tendency when judging such individuals to look further back into their lives for any preonset indications of
mental instability (and it is usually not difficult to find such indications,
or so we think). In the end, Edith's uncertainty as to what political opinions she does hold becomes the novel's uncertainty in that sphere.
Hence, five years after *A Dog's Ransom,* the confusion Highsmith regis-
tered in that book with respect to the American political scene remains
as strong as ever. In the earlier book, the various conflicting positions
had been divided among a number of characters; in *Edith's Diary,* they
are combined in one, and the self-contradictions reflect not just Edith's
dilemma but the novel's larger problem in coming to terms with its historical moment.

Sanity, Madness, and the Family

Critics have been divided on whether or not Edith Howland becomes mad.[28] Some see *Edith's Dairy* as depicting Edith's loosening grip on reality and descent into madness. The onset of this is indicated by her fantasizing events—mostly with respect to Cliffie—in her diary to such an extent that by the novel's end, the diary Cliffie has gone to Princeton, married, had two children, and worked as an engineer in Kuwait while the real Cliffie has settled into the life of a semidropout, lives at home at the age of 27, shows no signs of changing, and is not too upset at his failure to actualize himself in any even vaguely middle-class way. On the other hand, Edith remains fully competent to care for herself (and Cliffie) right to the end of the novel. She does not seem functionally impaired.

The question of Edith's madness is not, however, crucial to Highsmith's achievement in the novel; in fact, in the end, the difficulty in finally determining whether or not she is insane adds to the novel's force, as it constantly prods us to examine Edith's behavior in the light of her objective material conditions, her "situation," as Beauvoir put it. To a neutral observer, Edith might just appear a little odd in her behavior. Interestingly, Edith's mental state is sometimes discussed by the characters themselves. Cliffie, for instance, realizes "since a long time" that his mother had been "a bit cracked" (*Diary*, 308). Edith herself, midway through the novel, thinks, "*I sometimes think I'm going a bit nuts*" (*Diary*, 146), which might well be taken as an indication of her *not* being insane. Last, Brett attempts to have Edith seek psychological help on several occasions. Yet, in terms of her actual behavior, there is, with two exceptions, very little that would justify their diagnoses. The first, although important, is also something that can be seen as a principled stance on Edith's part. It involves perhaps the most crucial aspect in determining individual sanity—that is, the money aspect. Brett has given Edith a significant amount of money, $10,000 and $14,000. Edith refuses to accept this money, tearing up one check and refusing to cash another. Yet Edith's behavior is perfectly understandable as a desire to declare her independence of Brett.[29]

A second reason we may be tempted to go along with the characterization of Edith as disturbed is the ideas she expresses. For example, she tells Gert about an idea she has for a game in which people will wear masks of the president and vice president at the inauguration and will be immediately shot, leading people mistakenly to think the actual officials have been killed. Suggestions such as this, as well as some of the political ideas discussed earlier, lead those around Edith to question her sanity. Yet lucid, if eccentric, opinions cannot be accepted as symptoms of insanity.

When Brett visits Edith with a psychiatrist for the first time, the results by no means indicate a loss of reality contact:

> "How're things really, Edie?"
> "Not too bad. Why?"
> "Cliffie doesn't look in the pink," Brett continued in a low tone. "Gert phoned me. She thinks—"
> Edith had suspected that Gert had telephoned. "Well, thinks what?"
> "Just that you're under a lot of strain just now. You never cashed the ten thousand, it seems."
> "No, thank you. I didn't want it. I also don't want any part of the fourteen thousand in the Dreyfus—just so there's no fuzziness in the future about that one.—I'm doing all right, Brett, if it comes to money."
> "But this silly job." Then he seemed to give that up. (*Diary,* 272)

The analysis, or description, of Edith's "madness" really never goes beyond this level. Here, we do not, significantly, get the psychiatrist's opinion.

Hence the main indications are two: the people around her (mainly Gert and Brett) and her diary. Indeed, the diary is the only objective fact of Edith's "madness." Yet, as objective fact, it occupies a kind of no-man's-land. It is seen by no one other than Edith and, quite importantly, the fact is that Edith is perfectly aware that the dairy is a fantasized representation of her life (as well as of Cliffie's). As Klein notes: "The diary entries, which seem to demonstrate Edith's decline, are actually very carefully introduced, making clear her awareness of the life she is creating for herself. . . . While she does not consistently insist on this fictive approach, occasional reminders do surface to alert the aware reader of the deliberate and conscious creation of an alternative reality" (Klein, 185). Thus, Edith has not lost touch with reality. She is merely fantasizing about it, a perfectly normal activity, and writing down those fantasies, a less normal activity. Clearly the process of writing them down objectifies them, but it is still this side of acting them out. The primary content—and distortion of reality—of the diary is that her son Cliffie has achieved a successful middle-class existence: graduated from Princeton, become an engineer, married, had two children, and is working with American construction companies abroad. In this last datum, we have one of the most revealing aspects of the diary and something consonant with Highsmith's fiction as a whole: even in the fantasies of an eccentric protagonist, the isolated quality discussed in the last chapter, the centrifugal dynamic inherent in the Highsmithian emotional constellation, comes to the fore. Even the imaginary Cliffie and his imaginary family are not close to Edith (or to the United States—his last assignment is Kuwait). The tension between a drive for an almost indivisible unity and the distance deriving from an inability to tolerate emotional or even geographical closeness is central to Highsmith's world. On the one hand, we have, in reality, a Cliffie who cannot leave home, even at the age of 27, balanced by a Cliffie who seemingly finds it impossible to inhabit the same continent as his parents.

In the end, I think the novel is ambivalent about Edith's true mental state. There is the suggestion that Gert and Brett are, if not harassing Edith, at the very least overly intrusive. She has, to emphasize a crucial point, given absolutely no indication of an inability to care for herself and others. It might seem anachronistic to look back on Edith's predicament with the advantage of 20 years' hindsight of feminist discourse on the objective condition of women's lives. Yet 1977 was well into the second decade of second-wave feminism, and it is hard not to see Edith as being punished by society for her attempt to assert her independence of patriarchy. Whereas her refusal of Brett's money constitutes a basis for judging her behavior as inappropriate, in this very act, she most asserts her independence. In fact, when looked at as one in a gallery of female (or, for that matter, male) portraits drawn by Highsmith over the years, Edith is one of the most down-to-earth, realistic, indeed, *rational* of all Highsmith's characters.

A Note on Misogyny, Feminism, and Male Identification

It is hard to escape the negative impression of women that, although not without exception, is a continual presence in Highsmith's texts. Indeed, this stance was the provocative conceit of the collection of short stories *Little Tales of Misogyny,* first published in English in 1977.[30] Yet the gallery of negative portraits extends back to Miriam Joyce in *Strangers on a Train* and ends only with Renate Hagnauer in Highsmith's last novel, *Small g: A Summer Idyll.* Highsmith's response to criticism of her portrayals of women was consistent, if not convincing. When pressed on this issue, as she was numerous times, Highsmith gave one response: she identified with men because of their independence and activity.[31] When Joan Dupont asked Highsmith in a 1977 interview why she preferred men as heroes, she replied, "Women are tied to the home. . . . Men can do more, jump over fences."[32] A decade later she told the same interviewer, "Women are tied to the home, tied to somebody, not as independent to travel. . . . Men can do more, like jump over fences" (Dupont, 64). In 1993 she told Christa Maerker, "I can't imagine that women can summon up such physical strength to use a knife [as a weapon]. . . . Honestly, I just think men are more active. I have to confess, that's what I think" (Maerker, 153). Summing it up in *Plotting and Writing Suspense Fiction,* Highsmith wrote: "I prefer the point of view of the main character, written in the third-person singular, and I might add masculine, as I have a feeling which I suppose is quite unfounded that women are not as active as men, and not so daring. . . . I tend to think of women as being pushed by people and circumstances instead of pushing" (88). Perhaps her strongest antifeminist statement came in her interview with Bettina Berch in which Highsmith said that she saw women "as a bunch of pushovers, for the most part. I see them as whining, to tell you the truth. Especially this feminist thing—whining, always *complaining* about something. Instead of doing something" (Berch, 10).[33] Yet all this begs the question of why women are portrayed negatively because a number of Highsmith's female characters are, in point of fact, quite active.

We may grant Highsmith the truth of her self-analysis, but we have to examine its causes. Her identification seems to reflect one of the classic defense mechanisms, the internalization of the aggressor, according to which we "think" (with the "logic" of the emotions) that by assuming the ideas of the more powerful aggressor, we assume their power as well. Clearly for many women of Highsmith's generation and background, identification with the male power structure was something of a fait accompli. Highsmith reflects the ideas of the society she grew up in. Indeed, one might legitimately speculate that one of the things that has so drawn film directors (exclusively male) to Highsmith's work is the patriarchal views it often embodies. For instance, negative depictions of women are not foreign to a number of Hitchcock's films (nor, it might be noted, to those of his disciple Brian de Palma), including *Strangers on a Train.* But a writer does not exist in a vacuum. As the socioeconomic status of women in society changed in the 1970s, as "this feminist thing" gained strength, Highsmith's depiction of women changed significantly. Both *Edith's Diary* and *Found in the Street* reflect these changes in their positive portrayal of women.

Chapter Five

The Gay and Lesbian Novels

The novels of Highsmith's last decade (with the exception of *Ripley under Water* [1991]) are notable for their open treatment of homosexuality. In *Found in the Street* (1986) and in her last novel, *Small g: A Summer Idyll* (1995), Highsmith dealt with the topics of homosexual relationships and homosexuals in society. And in 1991, with the republication of her 1952 novel *The Price of Salt,* she acknowledged her authorship of that book. Although strict adherence to chronology would dictate discussing that novel in chapter 2, it makes more sense to treat it here. In its earlier incarnation, it led a subterranean existence as a lesbian classic, and Highsmith did not return to homosexuality as a subject for more than three decades.[1] Moreover, discussing the three novels in the same context more clearly reveals the effects of the movement for gay liberation. Last, the afterword Highsmith contributed to the 1993 edition of *The Price of Salt* provides a link from her early effort to her later—and then final—treatments of the theme.

The Price of Salt (1952)

Quite obviously, *The Price of Salt* occupies an unusual position in Highsmith's oeuvre. First, it treats lesbianism in a straightforward, aboveboard, and positive manner. Second, although such subject matter was marked for its era, the novel's technique—plot, characterization, and style—is the most conventional of Highsmith's 22 published novels and creates the most effectively realized pair of lovers in her fiction. But different as the novel is from what preceded and succeeded it, it still shows tendencies that we see developed in the rest of her novels. In the afterword Highsmith wrote in 1989 (published in the Naiad Press reprinting of 1993), she explains her original decision to use a pseudonym (Claire Morgan): "*Strangers on a Train* had been published as 'A Harper novel of Suspense' by Harper & Brothers . . . so overnight I had become a 'suspense' writer, though *Strangers on a Train* in my mind was not categorized, and was simply a novel with an interesting story. If I were to write a novel about a lesbian relationship, would I then be labelled a lesbian

book writer?"[2] The result was that until 1991 most of Highsmith's
readers did not know that she was the author of a lesbian novel.

The plot of *The Price of Salt* is among Highsmith's least complicated.
The 19-year-old Therese Belivet is working as a temporary Christmas
rush worker in the doll department for Frankenberg's, a large New York
department store, when she is transfixed by a customer whom she
serves. She later sends a Christmas card to the customer, Carol Aird
(whose address Therese has because the purchase was to be shipped).
Carol responds to the card, and a relationship ensues. Carol is in the
midst of a divorce (the circumstances of which are only vaguely described) from her husband, Harges. A few weeks into Therese and
Carol's friendship, Carol suggests they take a car trip out west, in the
course of which they become lovers. They have, however, been followed
by a private detective, who has bugged their hotel rooms and collected
enough incriminating evidence to effect Harge's complete custody of
Carol and Harge's child, Rindy. At the end of the novel, after Therese
and Carol have returned to New York, Carol decides to sacrifice her
rights to her child for a possible life together with Therese. Many elements that I have noted in the other novels are present in *The Price of
Salt* as well: the existentialist influence, the characters' obsession with
control, the negative image of the family, the ambivalence about sex,
and the fascination of commodities. There is also, at the beginning,
what we might term an interest in social realism, which was not to
appear in Highsmith's novels again until the 1970s, and then in different form. Here, this form of social realism is depoliticized and becomes
something akin to a proletarianized version of Sartrean nausea, a reaction against the banal routine of everyday life.

As the novel begins, Therese is eating lunch in the company cafeteria
and rereading the "Welcome to Frankenberg" booklet. Although the
booklet describes the various benefits that accompany longevity as a
Frankenberg worker, to Therese, "The store was organized so much like
a prison, it frightened her now and then to realize she was a part of it"
(*Price,* 4). Therese's goal is to become a set designer, but even though
she has prospects and knows she will be at the store only for a short
time, she is depressed by her situation. At lunch she meets Mrs.
Robichek, a woman who has been working at the store for five years,
whom Therese has noticed before: "She remembered the face. It was the
face whose exhaustion had made her see all the other faces. It was the
woman Therese had seen creeping down the marble stairs from the mez-
zanine at about six thirty one evening when the store was empty, sliding

her hands down the broad marble banister to take some of the weight from her bunioned feet. Therese had thought: she is not ill, she is not a beggar, she simply works here" (*Price,* 6–7). One evening, after work, Therese runs into Mrs. Robichek on the way to the subway where, "[s]he and Mrs. Robichek edged into the sluggish mob at the entrance of the subway, and were sucked gradually and inevitably down the stairs, like bits of floating waste down a drain" (*Price,* 11). Mrs. Robichek lives alone in a shabby, not very clean, single-room apartment, "like the one Therese lived in . . . only much darker and gloomier" (*Price,* 11). Mrs. Robichek's life is a frightening proleptic image of what Therese sees in store for herself. Carol will take Therese out of this depressing life. The contrast between Mrs. Robichek's and Carol's ways of life is, I think, meant to be seen as a contrast between the "nausea" of everyday existence and the possibilities that open up when one decides to "choose" one's life. Only at the end of the novel, however, when Carol renounces her affluent lifestyle, does the choice (for both Carol and Therese) seem an existential one, rather than one taken for quite understandable material reasons.

Therese's chosen profession of stage design concretizes the obsession that is the most important dynamic driving the emotions and behavior of Highsmith's protagonists, the desire to control their environment, including their relationships with others.[3] This desire for control, for a kind of stasis, is nicely depicted during Therese's first visit to Carol's suburban New Jersey home. " 'What would you like to do,' Carol asked. 'Take a walk? Play some records?' 'I'm very content,' Therese told her' " (*Price,* 56–57).[4] Therese's pleasure in Carol's presence suggests something like nirvana. Her pleasure is not so much passionate enjoyment or warm intimacy as a state emptied of all discomfort, anxiety, and pain. Although this state changes as the relationship between the two women unfolds, it is never wholly absent. Carol, too, is not immune to such a desire, though in her case it seems more explicable as a defense against her strong desire for Therese. Whereas Carol does not seem to desire stasis, she too has ways of protecting herself lest life get out of control. Carol, as can many of Highsmith's characters, can be enthralled by objects. At one point, Carol "feel[s] like looking at furniture this afternoon. . . . In stores or at the Parke-Bernet. Furniture does me good" (*Price,* 98). Later that day, Therese and Carol go to Chinatown, where they "ducked from one shop to another, looking at things and buying things" (*Price,* 103). "It was," Therese thinks, "a glorious evening, a really magnificent evening" (*Price,* 104). It is also one of the rare moments in Highsmith's fiction when the bliss of shopping (or of commodity appreciation generally) is enjoyed à deux.

Carol's own commodification becomes clearer when she remarks of her husband Harge's choosing her as his wife: "I think he picked me out like a rug for his living room" (*Price,* 125); and at first Therese feels that Carol is treating her like "a puppy Carol had bought at a roadside kennel" (*Price,* 73). Yet the fixation on consumer products in *The Price of Salt,* although muted relative to its presence in other novels, still reveals its power at odd moments, as when Carol visits Therese in her apartment. Carol assures Therese that she will not always be living in such straitened circumstances: "You'll travel. . . . You'll see a house in Italy you'll fall in love with" (*Price,* 96–97). The odd quality of this assertion may not register immediately, but for one who is aware of the role things—not to mention houses—play in the lives of Highsmith's characters, such moments, which might almost be overlooked, suggest the strength of such a dynamic. Surely, when thinking of the almost limitless possibilities of an attractive 19-year-old woman's future, one thinks of the men, or in this instance perhaps women (but certainly people), that she will meet and possibly fall in love with. When one comes right down to it, Carol's substitution of the house is little short of bizarre.

But Therese's passivity is counterbalanced by an active component revealed in a number of her statements and thoughts and enacted most vividly through the novel's resolution. This active component is the emphasis placed on an individual's capacity to choose, unencumbered by constraints such as heredity and environment—indeed, in one instance, by the suggestion of the absolute nullity of biology. Such an emphasis is not surprising. For a novel conceived and begun in the United States in the late 1940s and finished by 1951, the influence of Sartrean existentialism would have been hard to escape.

In Therese's case, the attempt to escape determination of any sort is reflected in the virtual denial of her family. On their first date, Therese tells Carol "her life story":

> But not in tedious detail. In six sentences, as if it all mattered less to her than a story she had read somewhere. And what did the facts matter after all, whether her mother was French or English or Hungarian, or if her father had been an Irish painter, or a Czechoslovakian lawyer, whether he had been successful or not, or whether her mother had presented her to the Order of St. Margaret as a troublesome, bawling infant, or as a troublesome, melancholy eight-year-old? Or whether she had

been happy there? Because she was happy now, starting today. She had no need of parents or background. (*Price*, 43–44)[5]

Although such things matter a good deal, the author does not want Therese's attraction to Carol to be psychologized as deriving from a dysfunctional parental relationship or an unhappy childhood. But Therese is very much the product of a problematic family constellation. With no explanation, her mother placed her in a home at the age of eight, after her father died. Later, her mother remarried, had two more children, and offered to take Therese back, but Therese refused the offer.

In the end one is left believing that family history is quite significant and that Therese's denial of its significance is just that: denial and wishful thinking. But the denial is effective in another way. Though we may surmise whatever we wish regarding the motivations for Therese's behavior, her own parti pris for living in the present and the increasingly assertive role she plays vis-à-vis Carol do create the picture of an independent woman taking control of her life. Highsmith effectively presents a portrait of an individual—conscious of her history but not bound by it—who acts freely.

One of the achievements of *The Price of Salt* is the depiction of the changing relationship between Therese and Carol, especially as the shifting balance of power reveals Therese and Carol changing as the novel progresses, something in marked contrast to the typical behavior of Highsmith's protagonists. More frequently, her characters' pathologies intensify, but the characters themselves do not change—in a sense they just become more and more themselves. Here, not only do Therese and Carol change, but their change is a direct result of the growth in their relationship as well as a reflection of their changed socioeconomic status, that is, Therese's career success and Carol's divorce.

They meet when Therese is working behind the counter in the doll department at Frankenberg's. "Their eyes met at the same instant, Therese glancing up from a box she was opening, and the woman just turning her head so she looked directly at Therese. She was tall and fair, her long figure graceful in the loose fur coat that she held open with a hand on her waist. Her eyes were gray, colorless, yet dominant as light or fire, and caught by them, Therese could not look away" (*Price*, 31). Two points should be noted. First, there is Carol's pose—and that is exactly what it looks like, a model's pose. The fur coat held open with a hand on her waist is reminiscent of the sketches one sees in the newspaper ads of such stores as Lord and Taylor and Saks Fifth Avenue, with their suggestion of stylized sophistication and grace. Therese first sees Carol as a model, objectified—almost in a showroom: in point of fact, in a department store. And this facet of Carol, and of Therese's relationship to her, is underlined a number of times in the novel.

The second and not unrelated moment is suggested by the description of Carol's eyes as "dominant," hinting at the power struggle latent in their relationship. At the beginning—and well into their relationship—Carol "calls the shots." This is clearest during the trip out west, the core of the book. The trip is Carol's idea, she invites Therese along, they use Carol's car, Carol pays all of Therese's expenses, and Carol drives and decides where they go. More specifically, it is Carol who is always, not to put too fine a point on it, telling Therese what to do. Although not always formal commands, Carol's statements reveal who is in charge. In an Ohio hotel room, Carol tells Therese, "I think I'll wear my slacks today. Want to see if they're in that suitcase?" (*Price,* 171), and a moment later, "Darling, I forgot my towel. I think it's on a chair" (*Price,* 172). As Therese stares at the city out of the window of their Chicago hotel: " 'Why don't you ring for some cocktails?' Carol's voice said behind her" (*Price,* 174). Much later, in Denver (after they have become lovers), as they prepare to take a drive with Mrs. French, an elderly woman they have met, Carol instructs Therese, " 'Wear your suede shirt.' Carol took Therese's face in her hands, pressed her cheeks and kissed her. 'Put it on now' " (*Price,* 203). These last commands echo an earlier moment, just before the trip, when Carol suggests buying Therese a tweed jacket. To Therese's response that she doesn't "particularly need one," Carol replies, "But I'd particularly like to see you in one" (*Price,* 155). Such statements underline the fact that, at the beginning of their relationship, perhaps primarily owing to disparities in age and status, Therese appears something of an acquisition for Carol (*found,* after all, in a department store), an undervalued object whose true worth Carol was able to see, in essence, a bargain, an early example of that dynamic in Highsmith's fiction whereby people become commodified and objects assume human qualities.[6]

Nowhere is the issue of control more tellingly presented than when it is a question of the physical expression of the women's feelings for one another. And, unsurprisingly, it is through the development of their physical relationship that they change in other ways vis-à-vis one another. Early in their relationship, when Therese asks to kiss Carol good night, Carol refuses, saying, "I'll give you this instead," handing Therese a check for two hundred dollars (*Price,* 131). The oddness, indeed hostility, of this gesture (attempting to treat Therese as a purchase) reveals it as an attempt on Carol's part to remain in control. Later, commiserating with Therese over a lost job opportunity, "Carol's thumb rub[s] behind her ear" (*Price,* 155). Although Therese feels that Carol might be "fondling" a dog, the gesture is significant for being Carol's advance. And, crucially, it is Carol who decides when they become lovers.

Sex plays an important part in this novel and suggests larger truths about relationships. Therese has had sex with her boyfriend, Richard Semco, "three or four times," but in that odd trope of Highsmith's fiction, they have decided not to have sex again until they are married (although Richard does occasionally make advances). At one point Highsmith phrases the sexual relationship a little oddly: "She had tried to have an affair with Richard three or four times in the year she had known him, though with negative results. Richard said he preferred to wait. He meant wait until she cared more for him" (*Price,* 25). But when she thinks of her experiences again, it seems that "cared for him" is a euphemism for enjoyed having sex with him: "She remembered the first night she had let him stay, and she writhed again inwardly. It had been anything but pleasant, and she had asked right in the middle of it, 'Is this right?' How could it be right and so unpleasant, she had thought. . . . And the second time had been even worse. . . . It was painful enough to make her weep" (*Price,* 51). Richard Semco is often insensitive to Therese in their relationship, and it seems that he is not sensitive to Therese as his sexual partner either. In contrast, Carol, for all her dominance, *is* sensitive to Therese.

Yet in *The Price of Salt,* we also have descriptions of sex, and intimacy—between women—that are entirely without such negative characteristics, and without precedent (or recurrence) in Highsmith's fiction. The description of the dawn when Therese and Carol awake after the first night they have spent in the same bed is light-years apart from the anguish Therese felt when sleeping with Richard; to my knowledge, it is the most positive portrayal of sexual contact in all of Highsmith's fiction:

> Carol's fingers tightened in her hair, Carol kissed her on the lips, and pleasure leaped in Therese again as if it were only a continuation of the moment when Carol had slipped her arm under her neck last night. I love you, Therese wanted to say again, and then the words were erased by the tingling and terrifying pleasure that spread in waves from Carol's lips over her neck, her shoulders, that rushed suddenly the length of her

body. Her arms were tight around Carol, and she was conscious of Carol
and nothing else, of Carol's hand that slid along her ribs, Carol's hair that
brushed her bare breasts, and then her body too seemed to vanish in
widening circles that leaped further and further, beyond where thought
could follow. (*Price,* 180)

"Hair," "lips," "neck," "ribs," "breasts": The unequivocally positive valuation of the body in this passage is unique in Highsmith's fiction; none
of the forced quality, the fussiness or tentativeness, of her other descriptions of sex is evident here.[7]

The author portrays the relationship positively not just in the representation of sex but also in the depiction of intimacy, a part of, but not
subsumed, by sex. Just before Carol returns to New York, the two
women are in a hotel. Carol is about to take a shower when Therese
steps under it:

> "Of all the nerve." Carol got under it, too, and twisted Therese's arm
> behind her, but Therese only giggled.
> Therese wanted to embrace her, kiss her, but her free arm reached out
> convulsively and dragged Carol's head against her, under the stream of
> water, and there was the horrible sound of a foot slipping.
> "Stop it, we'll fall!" Carol shouted. "For Christ's sake, can't two people
> take a shower in peace?" (*Price,* 229)

Such openness and vulnerability are unusual in Highsmith's characters.
Absent is the convulsively cramped tension of her other lovers, a tension
that not only underlies but constitutes those relationships.

An openness to the dynamic character of life is one of the achievements
of *The Price of Salt,* and it is most obvious in the changed relationship
between Therese and Carol and in the novel's resolution. Owing in part to
a misunderstanding, Therese interprets Carol's behavior in New York as a
rejection of her. When Therese meets Carol on her return, Carol makes it
clear that she has given up her daughter, Rindy, because the price for visi-
tation rights—a promise never to see Therese again—was too high. Carol
has a job, plans to live in Manhattan, and suggests she and Therese live
together. At first Therese refuses, and as Carol becomes fully aware of the
shift in the relationship, her awareness is reflected in her face:

> And now she saw Carol's face changing, saw the little signs of astonish-
> ment and shock so subtle that perhaps only she in the world could have
> noticed them, and Therese could not think for a moment.

> "That's your decision," Carol said.
> "Yes."
> Carol stared at her cigarette lighter on the table. "That's that."
> (*Price*, 269)

But Therese is ambivalent and a little later finds Carol in a restaurant: "Carol raised her hand slowly and brushed her hair back once on either side, and Therese smiled because the gesture was Carol, and it was Carol she loved and would always love. Oh, in a different way now, because she was a different person. . . . Therese watched the slow smile growing, before her arm lifted suddenly, her hand waved a quick, eager greeting that Therese had never seen before. Therese walked toward her" (*Price*, 276). Here, in the last lines of the novel, we have an emphasis on change that gives the novel an unusual force and differentiates it from much of Highsmith's other fiction.

But just as important is the positive valuation of the lesbian relationship.[8] This is overtly thematized toward the end of the novel in a letter Carol has written and left for Therese to read when she returns to New York. Therese does not immediately find the letter, and this partially contributes to her feeling betrayed. In the first part of the letter, Carol explains that she has told the lawyers that she will not see Therese again in return for the right to see her child. (She later changes her mind.) The second point, however, is a defense of lesbian love, impressive for its nuanced treatment of the topic, a subtlety that we have been alerted to earlier when Carol described to Therese a brief affair she had with Abbey, a childhood friend. "But the most important thing I did not mention and was not thought of by anyone—that the rapport between two men or two women can be absolute and perfect, as it can never be between man and woman, and perhaps some people want just this, as others want that more shifting and uncertain thing, that happens between men and women" (*Price*, 246). This is an intriguing passage, both for the element of choice it implies in sexual relations in general and even more for the light it throws on the behavior of Highsmith's figures in other novels. The heterosexual relationships depicted by Highsmith often have the feel of one of the characters searching for some kind of "absolute and perfect" rapport but being undermined by "that more shifting and uncertain thing."

The Price of Salt is one of Highsmith's best novels. Because it was excluded from the canon of her writings until recently, it never received the attention that might have made of it a more important book. One must recognize, however, that had Highsmith originally acknowledged her authorship, doing so might well have affected her subsequent career negatively.

Found in the Street (1986)

In *Found in the Street,* one of Highsmith's more interesting late novels, she takes up the attempt initiated 34 years earlier in *The Price of Salt* to represent homosexuality, this time from an angle broader than that of a single couple, if not yet encompassing a gay milieu, a task she would undertake in her last novel. Yet *Found in the Street* also embodies the ambiguities and ambivalences in representing the topic that we have seen in earlier novels. Moreover, Highsmith continues to depict familial relationships as tenuous and problematic. An interesting aspect of the novel is that the gratuitous, impulsive, irrational violence that figured significantly in many of her earlier novels has been decentered and marginalized, not appearing until near the end of the novel, and then in diminished form.

The novel takes place in New York City, almost exclusively in Manhattan south of Fourteenth Street, primarily Greenwich Village. Jack and Natalia Sutherland are a happily married couple living with their young daughter, Amelia, in a Grove Street apartment given to them by Natalia's great aunt. Jack is a book illustrator, and Natalia works in an art gallery. They thus belong to that stratum of the middle class that Highsmith has always been most fond of depicting: educated, middle-class professionals who have some financial independence or wealth (here, free housing) and, though not independent artists, are nonetheless part of the creative world. Jack, although a successful illustrator, is a commercial artist, working on commission.[9]

Jack Sutherland makes the acquaintance of an attractive young woman, Elsie Tyler, a waitress in a coffee shop. Elsie is beautiful and possesses a joie de vivre and naive charm that heighten her physical attractiveness. Through Jack and Natalia's connections, Elsie becomes a successful model. Charming everyone she meets, Elsie seems assured of a brilliant career, but she is bludgeoned to death by a jealous former girlfriend of Elsie's former lover. An important role in the novel is played by Ralph Linderman, a security guard who becomes acquainted with Elsie after also having met her in the coffee shop where she worked. Ralph holds puritanical views on sex and labors under the illusion that Elsie is in danger of being debauched by Jack Sutherland (whose wallet Ralph had found and returned early in the novel—hence the title). His presence hovers around the edges of the action, and at times he becomes central through his pestering of Elsie, his badgering of Jack (with whom, at one point, he comes to blows), and his repeated attempts to convince the police that Jack killed Elsie. Yet, as with much of Highsmith's fiction, the novel's power lies in its oblique treatment of certain issues and the ambivalence that runs through their depiction, and I think the novel can be usefully discussed as it relates to two of these issues: the family and homosexuality and AIDS.

The Family

Although it is fair to characterize Jack Sutherland as happily married, it is also necessary to see this happiness as dependent on a marked suppression of his own desires. It is hard to think of a character in any of Highsmith's novels who is as tentative and tenuous in his relationship to his wife as Jack. He seems to be walking on eggshells, inordinately grateful for the slightest recognition from Natalia. Early in the novel, for example, on returning from Philadelphia, where she had visited a friend, Louis Wannamaker, Natalia asks Jack, "How's your work going?"[10] While Jack puts her suitcase in the bedroom, "[h]is heart was beating with a gentle and pleasant excitement. *How's your work going?* Jack had to smile. Half the time she didn't care, Jack felt" (*Found,* 22). Jack is always grateful for small favors from Natalia, crumbs of her affection. One evening, after receiving a call from Natalia informing him that she is at Louis's New York apartment and will be home later, he reflects: "He hadn't any idea when Natalia would be home, maybe at 10, maybe not until later. But she'd call him, and that was something" (*Found,* 147). Indeed, such has been Natalia's insistence on distance that when giving birth to their daughter, she had shouted at Jack to leave the delivery room (*Found,* 147). "If Jack had pressed too hard, Natalia would have walked out, Jack was sure. She still would" (*Found,* 148).

Another aspect of the marriage, and not unrelated to Natalia's dominance in it, is that Jack assumes the traditional woman's role: cleaning the house, preparing the meals, caring or arranging care for Amelia, and preparing Natalia's breakfast. When he, Elsie, and Elsie's lover, Marion, leave a party in the early hours of the morning and go back to the Sutherlands', Jack prepares breakfast while Elsie softly plays a cassette: "Jack got to work in the kitchen on the menu of Canadian bacon, English muffins and scrambled eggs. Marion helped. Jack ground coffee with a couple of dishtowels over the machine to smother some of the noise" (*Found,* 167).

Natalia, on the other hand, is the antithesis of the traditional wife: "Natalia detested sewing on a button, and would rather wear a suit or a coat with a missing button for a week than pick up a needle" (*Found,* 132). Indeed, Natalia's presence is more a determining absence: she comes home late, is away visiting her friend Louis, is away visiting Elsie vacationing in New Jersey, stays at parties while Jack goes home. Her appeal for Jack is as much for her "objective" value—the way she has with commodities (much like Melinda's appeal for Vic Van Allen in *Deep Water*)—as it is emotional: "He was admiring Natalia's handsome, unpretty face, her special style in the black satin blouse which she'd taken from the house to wear" (*Found,* 61).[11]

Hence, the picture of familial relations the novel portrays suggests the delicate balances and careful calculations (at least on the part of one spouse) necessary to keep the institution of marriage afloat. Yet by the very fact that the family stays afloat, this depiction is more positive than in earlier novels such as *Deep Water* (1957), *A Dog's Ransom* (1972), *Edith's Diary* (1977), and *People Who Knock on the Door* (1983). There are, however, two significant conditions suggested by the Sutherlands' happy marriage, and these conditions relate to the question of reproduction (in both the biological and the economic sense) and indicate certain limits and qualifications that the novel sees as necessary to the institution's success.

In the first place, the family is not founded on a strict heterosexuality. Natalia Sutherland becomes sexually involved with Elsie, and that this involvement does not threaten the Sutherlands' marriage is due to Jack's tolerant, indeed, embracing, attitude. One evening, for example, Jack has returned to their apartment while Natalia is still out and goes to sleep not knowing where she is or when she will return. By now, he has become aware of Elsie and Natalia's interest in each other.

> And Elsie and Natalia? Now that was a surprise! What were they up to? Natalia had stayed out late a few evenings lately. Had she really been with Isabel Katz or with one of their art buyers?
>
> Jack went to bed feeling happy, and fell asleep at once. (*Found,* 170)

Hence, rather than being disturbed by the possibility of his wife having an affair with a woman, he is calmed by it. A little later, when Marion, Elsie's lover and roommate, informs Jack of Elsie and Natalia's increasing involvement with each other and says to Jack, "Hope it doesn't bother you," Jack replies, "No.—not at all" (*Found*, 188). Indeed, when Jack and Natalia are planning a vacation in Greece and Yugoslavia, Jack "half-expects" Natalia to suggest inviting Elsie along. "In fact, Jack wouldn't have minded. He could imagine himself sleeping in Elsie's hotel or pension room now and then, while Elsie spent the night with Natalia. The idea made him smile" (*Found*, 211). Jack seems remarkably self-effacing, even expecting Elsie to replace him in "his" bed, rather than expecting Natalia to go to Elsie's room.

A second restriction placed on the possibility of the family involves the question of the reproduction of domestic life. The Sutherlands have a young woman graduate student, Susanne, who serves as a combination nanny and domestic for them. With the odd hours the Sutherlands keep, Susanne is a necessity and is virtually on call 24 hours a day. Hence the child never creates the constraints on time and money that children usually do. Indeed, at one point, Jack does not even know whether Amelia is in the house or not. Susanne, as a denial of the real constraints of family life, functions similarly to Madame Annette in the Ripley novels, but here (the Ripleys are childless) as nanny as well. By employing Susanne, the Sutherlands evade the real demands of child rearing and hence, because her service elides one of the primary effects of reproduction, avoid an important issue.

The conclusion that we finally draw from this portrait of Jack and Natalia Sutherland's marriage and family is that such constellations have little chance of surviving unless they provide one member with a large amount of independence (a point Highsmith was to make again in her last novel).

Homosexuality and AIDS

The second major theme concerns the twin issues of homosexuality and AIDS, yet in diametrically opposed ways. Although homosexuals are a significant presence in *Found in the Street*, they are presented as scarcely differentiated from the straight community, and AIDS is mentioned, I think, only once in the entire novel. But the strong homosexual presence is misleading. There is, in point of fact, little about the gay characters that is identifiably gay other than the narrator's identifying them as such. There are two homosexual "sets" in the novel. One centers around Louis Wannamaker, an upper-class man who lives with his lover, Bob Campbell. They have a very conventional relationship, and little about them suggests that they are gay. They have separate bedrooms, and the sexual nature of their relationship is never mentioned. Twenty years earlier, their relationship would have remained in the closet. When Natalia goes to parties at their place, she says of them: "We don't talk about sex—or tell jokes. . . . In fact there's more talk about sex and more advances made at straight parties, if you ask me" (*Found*, 68–69). On the other hand, the openly gay milieu, that of Elsie, Genevieve (the woman with whom Elsie is first involved in the novel), and Marion, is presented as veritably all-American. "Genevieve's got a nine to five job! And I go to work before six today" (*Found*, 84), Elsie states at one point, irritated at Ralph Linderman's pestering her. The effect is to present homosexuals as no different—their object choice aside—from heterosexuals. It is essentially a conservative view of the issue (similar to the liberal view of the 1950s and 1960s), running counter to that of the identity politics of the late 1980s and early 1990s. Yet this is the view that Highsmith has chosen to represent in *Found in the Street*. No one is acting up here.

However, there is one significant aspect of the novel that, because it is suppressed, would seem to suggest that this view is not without its ambivalence. This relates to AIDS and is materialized through Louis Wannamaker's death, although Louis does not die of AIDS but commits suicide after learning that he has cancer. Yet the depiction of Louis's death strongly suggests to me that what is being (un)represented is an AIDS-related death. In the first place, Louis's disease has remissions; he lasts for months and, indeed, dies not of the disease but of suicide. Louis's lingering disease, with its period of remission, fits the profiles of both AIDS and cancer. But what is most striking about his death is the way in which it is handled by his lover, Bob Campbell, and by his friends, including Jack and Natalia. After finding Louis dead, Bob does nothing, neither notifying the police nor calling an ambulance, and the body is almost smuggled out of the apartment. Only after Bob calls Natalia and she comes over and suggests calling the police is Louis's death acknowledged.

> "Bob told me Louis wanted no ceremony at all, just cremation," Natalia said. "All written in his will. And Bob doesn't want us to tell people—just now. He'll see that there's a little item in the *Times*."
> Funny, Jack thought, though he said nothing. Awkward, too. The news of Louis's death would creep from friend to friend until everyone who cared knew it, he supposed. (*Found*, 181)

It is as if something shameful has happened, and although one might attribute this to the fact of suicide, that does not seem to me convincing; it does, however, fit a not uncommon mid-1980s reaction to an AIDS death.

One then asks why an AIDS death would be so threatening as to cause Highsmith to sidestep the issue and treat it in the way I think she does, especially in a novel whose protagonist is gay. If it is something so abhorrent, why introduce Louis's death at all? I think Highsmith was caught in a bind. Having committed herself, at least in substantial part, to treating a gay milieu in mid-1980s New York City, indeed, in the West Village, there is pressure to present what was a significant, even defining, moment in that community. Yet such is Highsmith's ambivalence that depicting AIDS, a condition often closely connected to homosexuals who have many sexual partners, would pose a problem for any attempt to present gays as different without differences, if one may so put it.

The treatment of Elsie's murder provides a further indication of the difficulty Highsmith would have had, had she tried to depict, in any detail, the gay milieu of the 1980s in New York. I noted earlier that gratuitous violence has here been reduced in its importance. Elsie is murdered by Fran (a former lover of Genevieve's), who is jealous of Elsie for having taken away her girlfriend. The murder is impulsive in that it was not premeditated, but it is not gratuitous, that is, unmotivated, because it arises out of jealousy. But there is a further point to be mentioned. Although most violence affecting homosexuals springs from the homophobia of heterosexuals, there also exists an *image* of violent, sadomasochistic male homosexuals that became notorious and widespread with the 1980 movie *Cruising* and was heightened by the later controversy surrounding some of Robert Mapplethorpe's photographs. Highsmith's depiction of Elsie's death at the hands of a lesbian is thus at least two removes from reality: the murder involves lesbians, rather than male homosexuals, and intrahomosexual violence, rather than the homophobic violence of straight males. This misrepresentation of reality would seem to suggest a mild antipathy or unease toward the milieu that Highsmith has—at least ostensibly—been painting in such "normal," even flattering colors. There is clearly a level on which her ambivalence toward that milieu remained unresolved.

This problem can also be seen in the depiction of Ralph Linderman. Ralph is reminiscent of Kenneth Rowajinski, the proletarian of *A Dog's Ransom,* who invaded the settled bourgeois existence of Ed and Greta

Reynolds. But the "threat" Ralph represents has been displaced, and he represents not a class but rather a cultural *ressentiment*. His puritanical worldview is such that he completely misreads Elsie, seeing her as possibly sexually promiscuous or even as prostituting herself. It is not until after she is killed that he begins to realize that she had relationships with women. What disqualifies him, in the context of the 1980s, from a more central role is his old-fashioned puritanism, something clearly out of place in 1980s New York. In this he is of a piece with the fundamentalist father of Highsmith's immediately preceding novel, *People Who Knock on the Door* (1983). The clichéd quality of Ralph's obsessions is clearly unusable at the historical moment of the novel, and this is tacitly recognized by the author as Ralph's presence in the novel becomes less and less intrusive. We might rather have expected Highsmith to show him as homophobic, and by depicting him negatively to be negatively portraying homophobia. But this she does not do. Indeed, it was not till almost a decade later that Highsmith addressed the issue of homophobia through the figure of Renate Hagnauer in *Small g: A Summer Idyll*. Yet the reduced threat of Ralph also owes something to the changed politics of the 1980s, quite different from the politics of the early 1970s reflected in *A Dog's Ransom*. Ralph, who works as a security guard, is very different from the disabled Rowajinski, who represented a class threat. Whereas Rowajinski attacked the property of the middle class, Ralph has settled nicely into his service-sector niche, content to protect the property of the propertied. Indeed, in the Reagan 1980s, the threat to that property has been so reduced that an attempted robbery of the parking garage where Ralph works fails.

A final point about *Found in the Street* is worth noting. In its representation of society, it is the most decentered of all Highsmith's novels (despite its tightly localized geography). This is a world in which there is no such thing as a "routine." Not only have sexual and familial relationships changed significantly, but society as a whole has no even keel. This is nowhere more clearly illustrated than in the fact that no one in the novel works regular hours. Ralph works the night shift at the parking garage and has to sleep at odd hours of the day; Jack Sutherland's work fits into the interstices of whenever he is not shopping, jogging, or taking care of Amelia or Natalia; Natalia's hours at the art gallery she comanages begin late in the morning and do not end at any specific time; Elsie works nights at the coffee shop; Louis does not work; Bob Campbell's hours are unspecified; and Susanne—working on a perpetual doctorate—seems to be on call 24 hours a day to take care of

Amelia. Although it is certainly true that work hours had become more flexible and contingent labor had increased in the 1980s, Highsmith's choosing to focus on this to the exclusion of all else, along with the importance that nontraditional roles and relationships play in the novel, creates a society in which everyone is marginal.

A Note on *Small g: A Summer Idyll* (1995)

Highsmith's final novel is noteworthy for its extended treatment of a broad, predominantly gay milieu. In *Small g,* perhaps not accidentally, she continues the kind of decentered depiction of social life that I have explored with respect to *Found in the Street*. "Small g" is a Zurich café, and the derivation of the name is explained several times in the novel. In a Zurich guidebook, a lowercase *g* prefaced to establishments denotes that they are not exclusively gay but cater to a mixed clientele of gays and straights. In conjunction with the novel's conclusion, we may, in this tolerantly mixed gathering place, justifiably read Patricia Highsmith's suggested resolution of the issue of sexual orientation as well as an attempt at creating a broader community, generally, than the relentlessly individualistic ones she had earlier depicted.

I do not think Highsmith ever wrote a novel (with the exception of *The Price of Salt*) to which the word "odd" could not be justifiably affixed. This is certainly one of her achievements. But for those who appreciate the niceties of her accomplishment, *Small g* might well be seen as constituting an oddity all its own. The novel has the feel of a late chamber work, say a piano quartet opus 125, but with the different parts not as hierarchically composed as is usual for the form and with something of an ambiguous tonality to it, at times verging on the atonal. This comparison is not entirely fanciful. Plot is as necessary to a certain kind of novel (Highsmith's kind of novel) as an assured key is to certain types of classical forms, and in *Small g,* we have Highsmith's most plotless creation.

Rickie Markwalder is a freelance commercial advertising artist, 46 years old. About half a year before the events of the novel, he lost his much younger lover, Petey Ritter, who was gratuitously stabbed to death as he was being mugged one midnight in January in Zurich (the brief first chapter describes the murder). Rickie becomes friendly with Luisa Zimmermann, who had been in love with Petey. She is an apprentice couturier who lives with her boss, the prudish and old-fashioned couturier Renate Hagnauer. One night at Jakob's (the formal name of the Small g), they meet Teddie Stevenson, a handsome (and straight) young man, who is quite taken with Luisa. Renate Hagnauer, repelled by and at the same time interested in homosexuals, assumes Teddie to be gay, and when a friendship begins to develop between Luisa and Teddie, Renate thinks that Luisa is once again setting herself up for a fall by becoming involved with a gay man who will only rebuff her overtures. Indeed, it has taken Luisa a long time to recover from Petey Ritter's death, in spite of the fact that they had only one date and he told her he was not interested in women.

Teddie, however, is not gay and pursues a relationship with Luisa despite Renate's attempts to thwart it. Because Luisa has run away from a former apprenticeship and Renate supports and vouches for her, Renate has a fair amount of control over Luisa, and the novel focuses on Luisa's attempts to achieve some kind of independence. At the end, a plan is devised to upset Renate so much that she will dismiss Luisa from her apprenticeship. One night, Luisa and Dorrie Wyss (a window designer who has become interested in Luisa) go to Luisa's room and get into bed together (keeping on only their underpants) and, though not having sex, make enough noise to awake Renate, who, seeing them in bed together, throws Dorrie out of the apartment. But while following Dorrie down the stairs, Renate trips, falls, hits her head on a banister, and dies. Subsequently, it is revealed that Renate has made Luisa a coheir (along with Renate's sister, who turns out to have died a year earlier, thus leaving Luisa full heir). Luisa inherits and continues to run the business with a coworker and a newly hired master couturier.

The novel is less eventful than this synopsis might suggest. Through its depiction of the intertwined relationships of Rickie, Luisa, Teddie, Renate, and Dorrie, the novel reflects the effects of the gay liberation movement of roughly the last quarter century, or at least Highsmith's appreciation of the movement. Yet Highsmith was well into her eighth decade when the book was written, and it would be unrealistic to expect that her attitudes toward homosexuality, sexuality, and relationships generally would show that marked a change. The spatial compass of the novel is even narrower than that of *Found in the Street*. The focus is the stage of the Small g, where the characters come and go, meeting each other for beer, coffee, or a meal. Rickie's apartment, his studio, and Renate's apartment (where Luisa lives and works) are all within a few minutes' walk of the place, in a Zurich neighborhood called Aussersihl, some distance from the center city. Although the surface of the novel tries to cast a somewhat sunny light on gays and lesbians, the typical

Highsmithian displacements and evasions suggest a fundamental problem with issues central to the novel.

Once again, as in *Found in the Street,* we have a distinctly odd treatment of HIV and AIDS and of homosexuality. Unlike in the earlier novel, the topic of AIDS is not—apparently—avoided. We are told that Rickie Markwalder is HIV positive. At one point in the novel, he goes to bed with a gay policeman, who is also HIV positive. Later on, however, we learn that Rickie is *not* HIV positive. His doctor had lied to him about the results of a test in order to force him to practice safe sex. "I confess I wanted to give you a real shock. . . . For your own good. I wanted you to find out you can live with 'safe sex,' if you understand me."[12] The doctor's logic seems far-fetched, not to say loony, because someone who is HIV positive might be inclined to more risks, not fewer. It then turns out that Freddie, the gay policeman, had also lied (to get Rickie to go to bed with him after Rickie had told *him* he was HIV positive). This incredible scenario clearly springs from an inability of the narrator to confront the issues of AIDS and, I think, of sex as well; the wishing away of AIDS also entails (emotionally, if not logically) a kind of wishing away or effacement of the sexual activity that causes the disease. Although Rickie and Freddie twice spend the night together, there is no attempt to describe their sexual activity. Such an attempt, in fact, occurs only once, and significantly enough, the depiction is not positive. After Renate's death, Dorrie and Luisa are in bed together. Luisa is barely interested in Dorrie, "too tired," and the sex is interrupted by Luisa's memories of child abuse by her stepfather. Although the history of abuse may be viewed as Highsmith's attempt to "motivate" Luisa's behavior, in the context of the text's overall inability to treat sex positively, it can more validly be taken as one more expression of this failing. Indeed, the closest relationship in the novel is between Rickie and Luisa. It is also the furthest from being sexual, as Rickie is a gay man and Luisa a bisexual woman. At the novel's end, she is described as occasionally going to bed with Teddie Stevenson and occasionally with Dorrie. Hence we have as the novel's "idyll," a community of relatively asexual individuals who, though "gay," "bi," and "straight," are really not complete individuals.

The most powerful figure in the book, and the threat to this community, is Renate Hagnauer, and she is also the focus of several displacements. She is something like an updated version of Ralph Linderman in *Found in the Street,* but she is still a little out of place. Upset at what she sees as Luisa's growing involvement with Teddie, Renate manipulates

Willi Biber, a large, mentally deficient individual, to assault Teddie one night as he leaves the Small g and goes to his car. Willi strikes Teddie with the iron leg of a tripod, causing a severe bruise and incapacitating him for a few days, though he fully recovers. Renate's hostility is strong, yet misplaced. Much as Ralph Linderman in the earlier novel felt he was protecting the lesbian Elsie Tyler from a heterosexual seduction, Renate feels she is protecting Luisa (who is apparently bisexual) from getting involved with a homosexual, which can end only in grief for her, as it had with Petey Ritter. But Teddie is not gay. As in the earlier novel, one senses that it is sex that is evoking these puritanical figures. But this is something the text would have trouble presenting in a straightforward manner, and thus this dynamic becomes displaced in the odd ways it does. The most intimate moments are never sexual.

But it would be a mistake to leave the matter there. These anachronistic and unrealistic figures function as powerful intrusions into the text. In *Small g* Renate is an imposing figure. The others pale in comparison, and hence her death comes as a shock to the reader and seems one of those moments where an effect beyond authorial intention was achieved. After all, in her mind, Renate was acting to protect Luisa (to whom she had willed a considerable sum), and Luisa had less than six months to go on her term of apprenticeship. Was Renate such a threat? Inevitably, her death seems unjust. Moreover, that her death results from what is seen as a lighthearted prank on the part of Dorrie and Luisa seems to be calling into question the values of the Small g milieu.

With its evasions, displacements, and low-key style, *Small g* is a somewhat odd end to a writing career and thus appropriate for Highsmith's career. Odd, and also evasive, was an American publisher's rejection of the book on the basis of its supposed offensiveness to "the lunatic right-wing fringe."[13] Highsmith's novels, however, have not always sold well in the United States, and one suspects that the rejection was motivated not so much by the fear of conservative reaction to the novel's "immorality" as by the fear of small sales—the ultimate immorality. Yet for the American author who expatriated herself to Europe for most of her adult life, whose novels often dealt in evasions of various sorts, this last European success and American failure seem a not altogether unfitting conclusion.

Chapter Six
The Short Stories

Highsmith's stories vary more than do her novels. Early stories such as "When the Fleet Was in at Mobile" or "The Heroine" (in her first collection, *Eleven* [1970]) are reminiscent of Carson McCullers. On the other hand, several of her collections are built around a central conceit: *The Animal-Lover's Book of Beastly Murder* (1975), *Little Tales of Misogyny* (1977), and *Tales of Natural and Unnatural Catastrophes* (1987). Whether formulaic or not, however, most of her stories have little in common with the mainstream American short story, regional or national, whether the southern gothic of McCullers, the *New Yorker* stories of John Cheever's buttoned-down WASPs, or John Updike's slightly more downscale and considerably less repressed suburbanites. Even less do Highsmith's stories have in common with Bobbie Ann Mason's or Raymond Carver's little-magazine story of the 1970s (which in turn metamorphosed into the *New Yorker* story of the 1980s), whose consumers are more likely to shop at Kmart (now, perhaps, at Wal-Mart) than at Abercrombie and Fitch. As is true of Highsmith's novels, the best of her stories possess an uncanny ability to enact certain moments of unexplainable individual anxiety ("The Terrors of Basket-Weaving") or to reflect socioeconomic changes as they affect that free-floating urban middle class in which she often sets them ("The Network"), in both cases with remarkably unsettling results for the reader. In my view, her two strongest collections are *Slowly, Slowly in the Wind* (1979) and *The Black House* (1981), and my discussion concentrates on stories from these two collections.

Slowly, Slowly in the Wind (1979)

"The Network" (1976)

"The Network" reveals some of the characteristics of Highsmith's best novels, enacting her oddly oblique representation of history and social change. Ideologically, the story complements *A Dog's Ransom* and highlights some of the issues treated in that novel. Yet, published some four years after the novel, "The Network" shows us a more one-sided version of that worldview, forgoing the attempt at reconciling the contradictions that made that novel an interesting, if flawed, achievement.

Fran Covak, a woman collecting disability from Con Edison, belongs to "the Network," which "consisted of a group of friends in New York who mutually bolstered one another's morale by telephoning, by giving constant assurance of friendship and solidarity against the sea of enemies, the nonfriends, the potential thieves, rapists and diddlers."[1] Fifty-eight years old, and unmarried, Fran's most prized "possession" is this network of friends. The son of a friend's nephew (but called "the nephew" throughout) arrives in New York to begin a career as a cabinet-maker. The Network attempts to help him obtain interviews and jobs, but he at first resists their aid, wanting to make it on his own. After he is mugged one night, however, he changes his mind and, with the aid of the Network, soon finds enough freelance cabinetry work to last him for six months. The story ends with him sending Fran flowers and apologizing for his brusque rejection of the Network's (including her own) offer to help him.

The slight tinge of racism and stereotyping that occasionally appears in Highsmith's fiction is here magnified, in part because the story is about the minority "threat." Of the Con Ed "inspector" who comes to check on the progress of her recovery, and for whom she "puts on a limp and a stoop," Fran thinks: "He was a black, though a nice enough type." Of a neighbor, she thinks: "Good old Harvey. . . . Jews knew how to do things. They were clever" (*Slowly,* 19). And, of the more general threat: " 'But nobody has to live in the *East Village,*' Fran said. 'They've got everything there, y'know, blacks, Puerto Ricans, spicks, just name it' " (*Slowly,* 25).[2] The tone throughout is of an environment become continually threatening:

> Somehow all the Network had fallen into Fran's habit of doubly verifying that their members were all right. Freddie was a commercial artist with a studio and apartment on West 34th Street.
> "Yeah, I'm okay. Say did you hear those police sirens last night?—No, not fire, police," Fran said. (*Slowly,* 17)

Yet although there is more than enough physical violence in the space of the story's 18 pages—a mugging and a violent assault (and attempted rape) that leads to eight stitches in the head of a young woman Network member—for this to be taken as the theme of the story, the obvious hyperbole of the Network's fears and of the events themselves undermines such a reading. The more resonant and authentic theme is the plight (and *ressentiment*) of the previously economically secure urban middle class, now fallen on harder times. It is a shabbier, frayed-at-the-edges, though still peculiarly Highsmithian, middle class of the 1970s, composed of Fran, who is "nothing distinguished, a secretary-accountant" at Con Edison for 17 years, a retired schoolteacher, a waitress, a "manager of a record shop on Madison," a theater designer (remnant of Highsmith's artsy Manhattanite of the 1950s), and "the nephew," a would-be artisan.

Fran Covak, the character from whose point of view the story is narrated, forms an interesting nexus in that she herself seems to be abusing her disability insurance as she criticizes the efforts of affirmative-action policies to mainstream blacks economically. Indeed, this is the crux of the matter. Early in the story, Fran receives an unsolicited call "from a mail order sporting goods store . . . on East 42nd Street, offering Fran a job starting Monday in their accounting department at two hundred and ten dollars a week take-home excluding their pensions and hospitalization plans" (*Slowly*, 18). Later, she tells this to Jane, another Network member, who remarks, "That means they've hired all the blacks they need to and they'd be delighted to stick in a white while they can" (*Slowly*, 19–20). What is striking about these moments is the contradictions they reveal. While collecting disability Fran is offered a better job than the one she has: in other words, her economic position remains privileged vis-à-vis that of minority-group members. The phone call from the sporting-goods store is completely unmotivated with respect to the story's ostensible theme and, indeed, would seem to contradict one of its corollaries: the depriviledging of the white middle class. Hence, this scene hints at the deeper tensions driving the story. Four years earlier, that tension had been present in the threat and class *ressentiment* of Kenneth Rowajinski, the proletarian of *A Dog's Ransom*, in Highsmith's distorting representation of the political and social movements of the 1960s. Here, the *ressentiment* has been transferred quite openly to the middle class, and the "threat" has been identified more openly as minorities. With Rowajinski, it had been marked as irrational; here it is construed as justified, although Fran is abusing her disability pension (which is nearly as much as her Con Ed salary), something Rowajinski was not doing. Yet her defense (though technically incorrect) is one of entitlement, as is clear in her conversation with Jane:

"If you don't feel like going to work yet, don't," Jane said, "Life's—"

"As *all of us* said once, if you remember, I'm only taking money that I've put *in* all these years. Same goes for hospitalization. Say, Jane, I don't suppose you could sign a paper or something saying you gave me a couple of massage treatments for the spine." (*Slowly*, 20, first italics mine)

Jane begs off as unqualified.

What is being enacted here? "The Network" is a story published in 1976, the year following the worst economic downtown in the U.S. economy since the 1930s. The secure independent income has now disappeared entirely, collapsed into Fran's tenuous temporary disability. Indeed, this causes Greg, the son of the nephew, to be referred to as "the nephew": the omitted generation that in Highsmith always marked the transfer of wealth, the provision of an (at least symbolic) independence, has here been collapsed into the third generation, which is thus left without money. The most the Network can do is to find him temporary *work;* he no longer has unearned income. The effects of a contracting U.S. economy, now beginning to affect the previously secure middle class, are being blamed on minorities. What is remarkable, however, is not the story's clumsy scapegoating, but how Highsmith, through the shifts, evasions, denials, and distortions—that is, the contradictions— effects a powerful impression of obscurely focused and oddly refracted, yet for all that quite real, anger. The attempt to fashion an old-boy/old-girl network of influence and support among this semimarginal group of "threatened" individuals elicits a pathos more effective than a more traditional social realism.

"Broken Glass" (1979)

In "Broken Glass," an oddly moving story, Highsmith again depicts the changed socioeconomic conditions of the 1970s. The story concerns the mundane life of Andrew Cooperman, a retired Brooklyn typesetter and a widower, as he makes his restricted rounds in a changing Brooklyn neighborhood. Muggings and burglaries at the hands of minority youth and the terror they inspire in Andrew's circle constitute the core of the story, a story, once again, expressive of that urban *ressentiment* noted even in the more secure Manhattan milieu of "The Network." Yet—also again—these preoccupations are seen through Highsmith's idiosyncratic sensibility, a lens whose angle is such that it poignantly distorts the phenomenon, capturing an aspect of it that is irrelevant yet revealing, though not of the phenomenon that is its ostensible subject.

On the surface the story is a piece of social realism (something "Those Awful Dawns" had attempted, though less successfully). The milieu is of aging, lonely people who have tenuous ties to one another and to no one else (their spouses have died and their children have moved away) and—for want of anything else—strong ties to their personal property (a subject that was treated more fancifully in "The Baby Spoon"). The characters are not affluent and thus continue the representation of mildly proletarian figures (for example, the proletarianized middle class in *Edith's Diary*) that had begun with *A Dog's Ransom*. Hence, we no longer inhabit the land of positional goods, the affluent suburban or exurban or (as in the Ripley novels) expatriated region where the consumer goods of the upper-middle class figure prominently. Andrew Cooperman's friend Kate is the widow of a subway guard, and it is the loss of her nice large television (now replaced by a smaller secondhand one) that is troubling.[3] Indeed, at one point in the story, it is suggested that the loss of such property is a fate worse than death.

These old folks are semihostages in their apartments. Andrew has not only "three locks plus a bolt and chain on the door" but "a big pine crate full of books and old magazines" because "Anybody could open locks these days, said Kate, and cut through a chain quick as a wink, but if they had to do all that plus push something heavy out of the way, it would give Andrew time to use his telephone. Kate could of course tell a story or two about a woman or man whose life had probably been saved and whose possessions certainly had by this precaution." To exit his apartment, Andrew has to "[tug] at his crate [to get] it just far enough away that he could open his locks and squeeze out himself" (*Slowly,* 164). Hence these old folks are twice held hostage by their possessions, the second time quite literally. Early in the story, an elderly couple, the Schroeders, are found dead in their apartment, where they have committed suicide. According to Kate, they killed themselves because "they couldn't take another robbery. They were too unhappy to go on. They'd had three or four, you know—" (*Slowly,* 166). Kate herself has suffered four burglaries: " 'What've I got left?' she asked rhetorically, rolling her head back so her eyes swept the walls, the sideboard on which a green vase stood (Andrew did remember a silver pot and teapot there years ago), the old second-hand television set where—was it four or even more years ago now?—Kate had had a big new set that she was quite proud of" (*Slowly,* 169). What is remarkable here is the extent to which things are seen as more valuable than people. People are transient, even though that transiency may last decades. Things—unless they are stolen—are not.

Andrew is mugged and a few dollars are taken from him, and a piece of glass he is using to frame a picture is broken. He is only slightly bruised by the mugging, and the next day, coming back with a replacement piece of glass, he sees the tall black youth who had mugged him (although the youth does not recognize Andrew). As the youth strides by, Andrew does not move and holds the edge of the glass so that the youth walks into it and is—effectively—stabbed in the stomach, though we do not know how seriously. Andrew himself has seriously cut four fingers but does not require stitches. At the end of the story, Andrew, again out on an errand, is slugged twice by the youth with what seems to be a heavy weight in a sock and dies.

On one level the story suggests that there is little hope for these oldsters, trapped in their declining inner-city neighborhoods. Yet the story seems so loaded with details that border on hyperbole (the pine crate, for one example, the suicides for another) that it fails in any attempt at typicality or realism. What it speaks to is a loss of status resulting from these individuals' loss of their consumer goods. It is no accident that in both "The Network" (where a mugging occurred) and "Broken Glass," the loss of economic status represented by the loss of goods goes hand in hand with the muggings. In the earlier story, the "enemy" had been affirmative action, a more mediated form of the redistribution of socially produced wealth; here the intensity of the conflict is more marked as the poor themselves effect the redistribution, and hence the violence has escalated several notches.

Both stories reflect the increased economic insecurity becoming visible in the United States in the 1970s as the costs of the Vietnam War and the decline of the real wage took effect. Yet these are phenomena to which Highsmith had earlier paid scant attention. What most struck Highsmith's sensitivities was the threat of radical social movements demanding genuine economic equality for minorities. A class position was being threatened. This is poignantly underlined by the fact that the piece of glass that Andrew has three times had to buy and leads directly to his death is to serve to protect the picture of his dead wife, representative of a happier, more peaceful, less-threatening time when radical social movements posed no threat to class relations.

Moreover, the suspicion that a class *position* is being threatened is literally and effectively underlined linguistically in these two stories by a striking description of the muggings. The phrase that appears four times is a variant of the muggers "sitting the victim down." When, in "The Network," Greg is mugged, "[t]wo fellows jumped on him and pulled his jacket over his head, you know, sat him down the way they do elderly people on the sidewalk, and took what money he had" (*Slowly*, 29). After Andrew is mugged by the black youths, he says, "I just got mugged, sat down on the—" (*Slowly*, 174), barely able to describe his humiliation; in an earlier mugging, "a younger boy had stood in front of him with a knife at the level of Andrew's eyes as he sat on the pavement" (*Slowly*, 175). Before he committed suicide, Herman Schroeder had been mugged, "and the boys had sat Herman down on the pavement" (*Slowly*, 166). The recurrent image suggests that these elderly people are being treated like children, put in their place, and is a poignant symbol of the author's involvement with them, of a powerlessness in the face of changed social conditions.

The Black House (1981)

"The Terrors of Basket-Weaving"

In the justly famous fourth section of the first chapter of *Capital*, "The Fetishism of Commodities and the Secret Thereof," Marx developed his classic analysis of commodity fetishism. "A commodity," he wrote,

> appears, at first sight, a very trivial thing, and easily understood. . . . So far as it is value in use, there is nothing mysterious about it, whether we consider it from the point of view that by its properties it is capable of satisfying human wants, or from the point that those properties are the product of human labor. It is as clear as noon-day, that man, by his industry, changes the forms of the materials furnished by Nature, in such a way as to make them useful to him. The form of wood, for instance, is altered, by making a table out of it. Yet, for all that, the table continues to be that common, every-day thing, wood. But, so soon as it steps forth as a commodity, it is changed into something transcendent. . . .
>
> A commodity is, therefore, a mysterious thing, simply because in it the social character of men's labor appears to them as an objective character stamped upon the product of that labor: because the relation of the producers to the sum total of their own labor is presented to them as a social relation, existing not between themselves, but between the products of their labor.[4]

Patricia Highsmith's short story "The Terrors of Basket-Weaving," the most uncannily moving she ever wrote, is a subtle and unsettling enactment of just how commodified human labor has become and how completely the social relations of commodity production have embedded themselves in our thinking. In the story, Diane (we never learn her last name), walking on a beach on Cape Cod, finds "a wicker basket bleached nearly white and with its bottom stoved in, but its frame and sides quite sturdy."[5] She decides to repair the basket, does so quickly and effectively, and then becomes so unsettled by its repaired presence that she winds up burning it after a week.

Diane first thought of repairing the basket because she "might use [it] to hold small potted plants. . . . One would be able to move several pots into the sun all at once in a basket" (*Black,* 50). At first, Diane is amazed that she has repaired the basket in less than 15 minutes: "How had she done it? She held the top end of the basket up, and pressed the palm of her right hand against the floor of the basket. It gave out firm-sounding squeaks. It had spring in it. And strength. She stared at the neatly twisted cord, at the correct over-and-under lengths, all about the diameter of pencils, and she wondered again how she had done it." It is at this point that "the terror beg[ins] to creep up on her" (*Black,* 51). The source of this terror, she thinks, might be that some atavistic ability has been revealed, something extending back millennia, in marked contrast to the skills required in her present job, for which, this weekend on the Cape, she had planned to write 300 words of a promotional brochure about

> a kitchen gadget that extracted air from plastic bags of apples, oranges, potatoes or whatever. After the air was extracted, the bags could be stored in the bottom of the fridge as usual, but the product kept much longer and took up less space because of the absence of air in the bag. . . . It was a sixteen-inch long tube which one fastened to the cold water tap in the kitchen. The water from the tube drained away, but its force moved a turbine in the tube, which created a vacuum after a hollow needle was stuck into the sealed bag. Diane understood the principle quite well but she began to feel odd and disoriented. (*Black,* 51–52)

Here we have the "transcendent" commodity par excellence, disorienting because it reflects how commodity-oriented a society we have become. As opposed to the basket, something that we can still imagine individuals producing for their own use value, we have a product, a "gadget" (the name suggesting something quasi-useless), that we could not imagine outside of a society whose economy is completely geared toward the production of commodities with "transcendent" value. Diane is aware of, and upset by, the contrast between the uses of the two products.

Yet the extreme alienation embodied in the kitchen gadget is, unexpectedly, less upsetting than the skill she has discovered in herself at basket weaving. Indeed, what troubles her is not only—and perhaps not so much—the fact that she has repaired the basket but the extreme speed and facility with which she has done so. She is frightened—terrified—at this residue of an atavistic manual skill.[6] Moreover, the effect of successful craft work so overwhelms her that it haunts her throughout the story, even after she has burned the basket. The basket was not a "transcendent" commodity; it was something produced solely for personal use, a usefulness that came directly from Diane's work on it, and this "terrifies" her, a word repeatedly used to describe her experience. Although she has trouble writing her 300-word blurb for the gadget, with respect to the basket, "Everything I did, I felt sure of" (*Black,* 54). During the following week, she feels "scared, mysteriously terrified," though only one untoward event occurs: "she . . . let one side of the lettuce-swinger slip out of her hand on the terrace, and lettuce flew everywhere." The lettuce-swinger represents another "transcendent" commodity, and the incident reveals Diane's fear of losing her grip on such production. The next weekend, flying with her husband to the Cape, she decides to "treat it like any old basket," putting any old thing in it. "That would take the mystique out of it, the terror" (*Black,* 57). The condition of the commodity that Marx had described, that "so far as it is a value in use there is nothing mysterious about it," has been turned on its head. Mysterious has now become its value in use.

Diane continues to feel upset, though, and even considers taking a month's leave of absence from her job. Her husband, Reg, says: "Really, Di, the leave of absence is one thing, but that basket—it's an interesting basket, sure, *because it's not machine-made* and you don't see that shape anymore" (*Black,* 60, italics mine). Finally she burns the basket, though "she was no happier now than during that week when the well-mended basket had been in her possession" (*Black,* 62).

Throughout this book I have noted the importance of things, usually commodities, in the lives of Highsmith's characters, especially commodities that function well. From Ripley's ecstasy at the package net in the Paris-Rome train, through the ever-increasing positional-good gifts that he purchases for Heloise, through the outsized importance of the "Vacheron Constantine" watch that David Kelsey forces on his friend Wes in *This Sweet Sickness,* such consumer goods exert a power on the characters that would be hard to overestimate and, through their omnipresence in the texts, affect the reader as well. Yet these objects are most usually "transcendent" commodities, tokens of alienated labor that in turn enslave. For this reason, the fact that Diane has become terrified of the one object that is, in its use value, a product of her own, noncommodified labor power is one of the most powerful indications of the extent to which the characters in Highsmith's fiction have repressed their own alienation. Were this not the case, Diane would be gratified, not terrified, at her skill, as an indication that this deeply embedded human ability has not been completely effaced by centuries of increasing commodification.

There is yet another source of Diane's terror, and it too reflects a basic element of Highsmith's characters, that is, their essential isolation from any broad human community. Indeed, such isolation produces a fear of human community, and we see it when she first recognizes her terror:

> That was when the terror began to creep up on her, at first like a faint suspicion or surmise or question. Had she some relative or ancestor not so far in the past, who had been an excellent basket-weaver? Not that she knew of, and the idea made her smile with amusement. Grandmothers and great-grandmothers who could quilt and crochet didn't count. This was more primitive.
> Yes, people had been weaving baskets thousands of years before Christ, and maybe even a million years ago, hadn't they?
> The answer to her question, how she had done it, might be that the ancient craft of basket-weaving had been carried on for so long by the human race that it had surfaced in her this Sunday morning in the late twentieth century. Diane found this thought rather frightening. (*Black*, 51)

The thought that there could be any kind of deep solidarity between Diane and others, especially other workers, is anathema to her. The underlying alienation from the social world (often enough including the world of work) is a strong force in Highsmith's fiction and is evident here in Diane's terror at the possibility that any kind of solidarity or community with others (if only of a symbolic nature) might exist.[7] This lack often finds expression through the absence of the parental genera-tion, as it does here with the reference to "grandmothers and great-grandmothers," but not to mothers. The skill with which Highsmith melds all these themes and uncannily causes the reader to feel at least some of Diane's inarticulate unease produced, in "The Terrors of Basket-Weaving," a small masterpiece.

The "mystery" that Marx had attributed to the commodity, because in it the social character of people's labor confronts them as an object *against* them, is reversed: production for use value alone—Diane's work on the basket—produces a "mystique" that terrifies. So alienated have we become that it is now use value, and all that it suggests about social life, that terrifies, and alienation—alienated labor in the form of the commodity—that reassures.[8]

"A Clock Ticks at Christmas" (1979)

The grip that objects have on us is also revealed in "A Clock Ticks at Christmas" (from the 1985 collection *Mermaids on the Golf Course*), whose plot is simple enough. Michèle, a Parisian bourgeoise, pities and befriends Paul, a street urchin who begs her for a "spare franc."[9] She makes him small gifts and invites him (and then him and his sister) into her apartment and feeds him. After the second visit, she discovers that a clock, a prized family heirloom of her husband, Charles, is missing. The marriage founders on the opposing views the spouses take of the theft: Charles finds it unforgivable, while Michèle sees it as understandable, given the child's poverty, and four months after the event, they divorce. The clock is never found.

The story takes place at Christmas, and it is no surprise that it focuses on things that money can buy. Indeed, the amount of purchasing that Michèle does at the beginning of the story is noteworthy even for a High-smith character. She notices Paul "over her armsful of boxes and plastic bags" (*Golf*, 91) as she is entering the court of her building. She has purchased a number of Christmas presents for Charles, her parents, a present for Charles to give to his parents, as well as a present for herself ("a Hermes belt she hadn't been able to resist" [*Golf*, 92]). Michèle personifies the consumption function, and in a way, she purchases Paul, too.

Indeed, the story makes clear that both Paul and Michèle are acquisitions. The second time Michèle encounters Paul, she is returning with a white poodle she has just bought. She invites Paul up to the apartment to play with the dog, and in four interactions that quickly follow one another on the same page of the story, it becomes clear that Paul and the dog are almost interchangeable:

> "What shall I name the puppy?" Michèle asked. "Any ideas? What's your name?"
>
> The boy and the puppy followed her. Michèle set down a bowl of water for the puppy, and took a bottle of coca-cola from the fridge.
>
> Slowly and steadily the boy ate them all, while he and Michèle watched the puppy licking the last morsels from his saucer. (*Golf*, 95–96)

She also gives Paul some of the same hamburger meat she feeds the dog. For Michèle, Paul is like a purchase just as she herself is viewed by Charles, her husband, as an acquisition. Charles, the head of a construction company (he has worked his way up from an apprentice mason), is from a poor family, and in Michèle, the daughter of one of his clients, he has married someone far above his own class (there are a number of oil paintings of Michèle's ancestors in their apartment): "Sometimes Charles felt dazzled by his success in his work and in his marriage, because he adored Michèle and she was lovely" (*Golf,* 92). Michèle's primary value for Charles is that of a beautiful object.

With the theft of the clock, the story shifts to another level. It is an ormolu clock, inherited from Charles's father, and although Michèle, in a vain attempt to deflect its absence, has put a gift-wrapped package in its place, Charles immediately notices that the clock is missing: " 'Something the matter with the clock?' Charles's face had grown serious, as if he were inquiring about the health of a member of the family whom he loved" (*Golf,* 102). Charles is so upset that he cannot go to the dinner party they had planned to attend that evening, and Michèle goes alone. At the party she confides to a friend what has happened. By chance there is a very similar clock, which the friend gives her to replace the one stolen. Michèle accepts the clock and places it on the mantel. When Charles spots the new clock, he "turned to Michèle with a shocked look in his eyes: 'All right, Michèle. That's enough.' " Charles, who has already notified the police (and given them a colored drawing that he had made of the clock at age 14), speaks to Michèle "in his tone of barely repressed fury, about dishonesty, hand-outs to the irresponsible, to those who had not earned them or even tried to, about hooligans' disrespect for private property" (*Golf,* 105). At first the issue seems merely the hard-heartedness of one who has risen through his own efforts versus the noblesse oblige of someone born to wealth and status. But later Charles refuses to go to his parents' house for Christmas dinner: "Do you think I can face my parents—admit to them that the clock's been stolen?" (*Golf,* 106). Still later he cannot even bring himself to meet Michèle at her parents' house. Michèle and Charles never reconcile their differences, and four months later they divorce.

What makes the story intriguing is Charles's passionate attachment to something that has so little value in the ordinary scheme of things. It cannot be the clock's usefulness or even its aesthetic value because he refuses an almost identical replacement. Rather, it is, as Michèle's mother remarks, "the sentiment" (*Golf,* 107). That is, the one object, in a story filled with objects, that is loaded emotionally is this relatively valueless clock. It is the one object of value that his working-class father was able to afford (as opposed to the veritable cornucopia of things with which Michèle enters her apartment house, none of which is identified except her own Hermès belt), and it is striking, indeed, that Paul would feel dishonored were his father to know that his one bit of accumulation had been lost. It had been Charles's family's "pride and joy . . . the one handsome item in their working-class household" (*Golf,* 103). Paul's overestimation of the clock devalues all the subsequent accumulation (including even Michèle) that he has achieved. The clock is the one thing that cannot be purchased, that escaped the category of commodity, because its value is one of emotion, not exchange value or use value. Hence, in a story where the protagonist seems almost to function primarily as a conduit for the purchases that she (and others) use to express their feelings for one another—lacking any other outlet—the one object that cannot be purchased becomes central to the characters' relationship. Moreover, *her* transgression was to also fall prey to her emotions, in her case, for the impoverished Paul. Because she comes from a wealthy family, things are not as important for her as they are for her husband, who comes from a poor family, and the result is that each spouse winds up identifying with the opposite class of their origin, and the story also suggests that this might have had something to do with their original attraction for each other.

"Blow It"

A similar problematic underlies the story "Blow It" (in *The Black House*) and is most usefully discussed in the context of the confusion of people and things central to "A Clock Ticks at Christmas." The story concerns Harry Rowe, a young man having trouble deciding which of two attractive girlfriends to marry, Leslie Marker, a photographer's model, or Connie Jaeger, an editor. Harry, an accountant and a lawyer, "really didn't know which girl he preferred" (*Black,* 189). He met both women around the same time, both women are 23 years old, and both women are interested in marrying him. Harry is "careful to keep the girls apart" (*Black,* 191), seeing them on different days of the weekend. As far as he knows, neither is aware of the other.

The situation becomes critical when Harry's friend and colleague, Dick Hanson, tells Harry of a house in his Westchester suburb whose owners are leaving. Harry can have the house at a good price, provided he decides soon, as the house will be given to a broker within a week. Harry lives in Greenwich Village, and Connie and Leslie also live in Manhattan. Harry "wouldn't want to move there alone" and realizes that the crucial moment is at hand: "Could Leslie live with him and still commute? At very early hours sometimes? She might not consider a country house worth it. Could Connie? Yes, more easily. She didn't have to get to work till nine-thirty or even ten. But a man didn't choose a wife for ease of commuting. That was absurd" (*Black,* 196). As he tries to decide, Harry's thoughts waver indecisively between the women. Even as he views the house with Dick Hanson, he continues to obsess:

> Wouldn't it be great to be master of such a house, Harry was thinking. And which girl would be mistress? He had a vision of Leslie walking through the door from the hall, bearing a tray of something, smiling her divine smile. And almost immediately he saw Connie strolling through, blonde, calm and gentle, lifting her blue eyes to meet his.
>   Good Christ! (*Black,* 198)

Harry lights upon a possible solution: "to speak to both girls and ask them straight out if they would like such a house, in such a location, and—either Leslie or Connie might say no" (*Black,* 198). But Harry cannot bring himself to take this step and winds up asking each of them to meet him at the house, almost at the same time: "He could see which girl liked the house better" because "He somehow had to confront both of them, and himself, with the Westchester house at the same time" (*Black,* 200). The inevitable catastrophe results, and both women break with Harry.

The story is a quirky and effective representation of a problematic that we have seen extending itself in various guises throughout Highsmith's work: the objectification of people and an almost pathological investment of emotional energy in things. What gives such representations their force is that although most people do not engage in such an overvaluation of things or devaluation of people, we can nonetheless see ourselves in Highsmith's characters. The house is a unique bargain in that Harry can have it for $90,000, whereas it will fetch $150,000 on the open market; on the other hand, the women are interchangeable— the same age, equally attractive, met at the same time. It is clear in the passage quoted that Harry sees the women as complements to the house, furnishings, as it were. In a society where so much has been com- modified in terms of exchange value (Harry sees himself as a "catch," which "meant, he was earning well" [*Black,* 189]), why not wives, too? And it would be silly to deny that the phenomenon exists (as, for example, when corporate executives are, in part, judged promotable based on the attractiveness of their wives). Yet Highsmith's representation is at best only peripherally concerned with this kind of social criticism. And in fact Highsmith is not being critical; indeed, the implied author's stance is remarkably objective, and it is by no means easy to determine which side "she" is on. Indeed, it is suggested that Harry is not alone in his situation. At the beginning of the story, we learn that Harry's friend, Dick Hanson (who apprises Harry of the house and through whom he can acquire it so cheaply), is "a thirty-five year old married man . . . [who] even now has a girl friend" (*Black,* 189). At the end, it is this same person who, after the fiasco, tells Harry: "They're both *lovely.* . . . I can understand your problem! Believe me, Harry! But don't give up. . . . Don't be silly," he says, in a peculiarly apt metaphor, "You can patch things up" (*Black,* 207).

"Old Folks at Home"

This story, perhaps deriving from the same experiences and feelings that produced the figure of the bedridden Uncle George in *Edith's Diary,* humorously reverses the behavior of the primary-care providers vis-à-vis their burden. In the story, Herbert and Lois McIntyre, a professional couple (he is a "strategy analyst," she a history teacher with "three books and a score of articles" to her credit) living in suburban Connecticut "adopt" an old couple who live in a nearby nursing home. Because "[t]hey had no children themselves, and didn't want any. . . . they felt a little guilty about not fulfilling their duty in this department." The reasoning behind the decision is presented as rational: "It was not a hasty decision on the part of the McIntyres" (*Black,* 136).

The adopted couple, Mamie and Albert, prove to be self-centered and become an increasing burden. They sit in their room all day watching the TV with the volume turned up, as Albert is hard of hearing, and being waited on for meals and "tea" by Lois. Soon, Albert becomes incontinent. The McIntyres try to return the couple to the nursing home, but the home is now full, and it is made clear that Mamie and Albert are now the McIntyres' responsibility. Worst comes to worst, and finally both Lois and Herbert have to rent separate offices in Hartford to work in during the day. After several months of trouble with the elderly couple, they return from their offices one day to see smoke billowing out of Mamie and Albert's upstairs room. The McIntyres rush in to save their own papers and books and, after some hesitation, decide not to try to save the old couple or even to call the fire department. They drive off to the house of friends, effectively committing the couple to their death.

Although the story has, for Highsmith, an unusual amount of humor, its point is serious and pessimistic. The McIntyres have tried to escape the bonds of the family (an institution that Highsmith rarely depicts positively). Their own parents are out of the way, 3,000 miles off in California. Yet an irrational need has caused them to "adopt." By adopting old people, they have effectively escaped the emotional bonds that cause so much grief for people and would have arisen had they adopted children (these old folks may well die at any moment). The "adoption" seems merely formalistic. Naturally enough, too, Mamie and Albert, having already raised a child of their own (also 3,000 miles away in California) are interested not in any emotional bonding but only in their own comfort. But in the end the McIntyres cannot escape the family and its costs (they are paying somewhat less than half the costs of the couple), even if the family is not their own. The family structure is so omnipresent in society, Highsmith suggests, that if we do not have it, we seek it out, inevitably discovering its horrors as well. The primary imposition lies in the McIntyres' inability to get any of their work done at home (child care, of course, is one of the primary concerns of working couples), and it is when they are forced out of the house that things come to a head and the ineluctable nature of the family appears. The McIntyres had wanted adults but wound up getting children. As one of their friends, commiserating with them, had asked: *"What if Mamie and Albert outlive you both?"* (*Black,* 158–59).

"The Black House"

"The Black House," one of Highsmith's most effective stories, is unusual in that it almost demands symbolic interpretation. It is not so much that the story operates on a consistently symbolic level as that from the beginning there is the strong suggestion that the story should be read on more than the literal level.

The black house is an abandoned house in Canfield, an old, unexceptional upstate New York town "composed of respectable middle-class Americans, many of whose families had been there for two hundred years" (*Black,* 229). Timothy Porter, who grew up in the community but spent a year away at a boarding school and attended Cornell University, has returned at the age of 23 to work in the town and live with his uncle, Roger, whose wife, Meg, has recently died. Dropping by the White Horse Tavern on several occasions, Tim invariably hears a group of older men talking about the black house and what took place there in their youth: it was there that they all had—or say they had—their first sexual experience with a woman. Intrigued by the tone in which they talk about the house, Tim visits it twice—though he has been warned by the men and his uncle after his first visit not to return. He does return, however, explores it thoroughly, and finds nothing exceptional in or about the house. After the second visit, he returns to the tavern and tells the men that he has explored the house and found "Just nothing. All quiet." One of the men asks, "What do you mean—nothing?" (*Black*, 246). Although all the men's responses differ, they are all uncomfortable in some way:

> Their expressions were a bit different, each man's, but in each was disappointment, a hint of disapproval, perhaps. Tim felt uncomfortable. Sam Eadie's face seemed to combine contempt with his disapproval. Ed's long face looked sad. Frank Keynes had a glint in his eye.
> "Nothing?" Frank said. "You better step outside, boy!" (*Black*, 246–47)

Frank repeats his command, and Tim follows him outside, where Frank assaults him, striking him several times. Tim lapses into a coma and dies three days later.

Tim had cast doubt on something that the men of the community cherished, although the women "chose to forget it, as if it were an eyesore that they could do nothing about" (*Black*, 229). It is clear that the visit to the house, in one's midteens, with a girl, represents sexual initiation. Although Tim has grown up in the community, he was away at the time when it was usual for men to make their visit and had visited the house only as a preadolescent of age 10. Membership in the fraternity of the tavern requires both marriage and a belief in the significance of the sexual initiation undergone at the black house. Tim's uncle, Roger, for example, a childless widower, does not associate with the other men at the tavern, and none of Tim's own relationships with women have led to marriage; indeed, at one point, he is attracted to a local woman in the bar but cannot even make her acquaintance.

But the specific meaning of the experience the men underwent at the black house is further defined by two incidents connected with it. The first, in its use of a modal auxiliary to express a customary event, suggests an archetypal aspect. It involves Frank Keynes, the man who eventually murders Tim:

> Another round of drinks—perhaps it would be "after church" at half past noon on a Sunday—and Frank Keynes would relate a story of when he was fourteen with a crush on a girl in school, and he'd made a date with her to meet at nine o'clock at night at the foot of the hill to the black house, and she had stood him up. "But what do you know? Along came *another* girl who was quite willing to go up to the black house. *Quite willing!*"
> The men would laugh. Was it true or not? (*Black,* 230)

Hence, it is suggested that the experience is not related to any particular woman, to an emotional bond, but rather solely to sex. Moreover, there is a valid question as to whether the events actually occurred or are merely male boasting.[10] The second incident concerns an adolescent boy who was murdered in the house. The boy had made a girl pregnant, presumably in the house. Indeed, "she and the boy had made a date to meet again—in that house. . . . they often met there. The story is that her father was furious" (*Black,* 234). Taken together, the two incidents reveal the house as the scene of sex. It is not the scene for emotional entanglements and all the less the locus for the formation of a family (as the boy finds out).[11] Indeed, the women the men have sex with in the black house do not "for the most part" become their wives (*Black,* 235).

This, in fact, is the prohibition that the black house enforces: sexuality, as a forbidden pleasure, is to be divorced from the family. This prohibition has been extended into adult life in that the men, sitting away from their wives (though their wives are present in the bar "out of hearing"), relive the illicit, sinful pleasure of sex qua sex (that is, sex not in the service of reproduction) by incessantly talking about their experiences in the black house (which they never talk to their wives about). This is revealed in a subtle linguistic usage. After the wives have allowed the men their (relived) sexual experiences, the wives come over to the bar, and as Sam Eadie puts it when he addresses Ed Sanders's wife: "I think you've come to collect" (*Black,* 231). The avoidance of the direct object allows us to take "collect" in two ways. Naturally, Sam means "to collect Ed and take him home." But the lack of the object also suggests that Kate Sanders has come to collect on her part of a bargain. The women have allowed the men to boast and fantasize of their sexual adventures, but it is now time for them to return to their roles as family men and faithful husbands.

Up to this point, the story can be read as adhering to one convention of American literature as convincingly described by Judith Fetterly in her book *The Resisting Reader*. Fetterly's interpretation of Washington Irving's "Rip Van Winkle" sees Rip's 20-year absence in the Catskill Mountains from his henpecking wife as archetypal of the American male's escape from responsibility and the depiction of his wife, and wives generally, as henpecking as archetypal of their consequent demonization. Rip is the boy always refusing to grow into and accept the responsibilities of adulthood. Indeed, as Fetterly puts it, "an essential part of the Americanness of Irving's story is the creation of woman as villain: as obstacle to the achievement of the dream of pleasure: as mouthpiece for the values of work, responsibility, adulthood."[12] Yet several things complicate such a reading of "The Black House." First, there is really no Rip figure in the story. The men have all settled down to married life, and Tim, though he has not, wants to. In fact, he is presented as in some ways more mature than the married men, and his absences have been for productive purposes: boarding school and university. Moreover, although the story does show the men as, at least in their own eyes, mildly henpecked, the women are not so much presented as shrews as given short shrift, generally. Moreover, the presentation of men is undermined by the doubt cast on their "exploits" throughout the story: are they mere boasts, or true experiences? This is never finally made clear.

Epilogue

It is hard to evaluate Highsmith's work by conventional standards. Her achievements cannot be easily categorized in traditional terms. She was not a striking stylist; her plots are ingenious, but plot is actually secondary to her achievement; in one sense, her characters are not memorable. One critic noted that we rarely remember what they look like. For example, I am always surprised on rereading *Deep Water* to discover—once again—that Vic Van Allen is somewhat pudgy. But then, the intensity of these conventional-appearing individuals is all the greater for their outward lack of distinction. In the best of her novels, what we recall is not so much the characters' person as the intensity of their problematic: Vic Van Allen's attempt (at least in his own mind) to achieve some kind of urbane triangle with Melinda and her lover (whoever that might turn out to be) or David Kelsey's perfect life with(out) Annabelle Stanton in his Ballard house. In this "Websterian intensity," as Brigid Brophy aptly termed it, Highsmith has managed to create an impressive number of times an intensity far different from what we usually expect, or get, in novelistic figures. Brophy's analogy aside, there is a monologic, rather than dramatic, atmosphere to Highsmith's protagonists. It is not so much that they live in their own world as they want to control access to the world in which they live.

Highsmith's evasions have contributed powerfully to the intensity that many readers have felt. I think this intensity stems primarily from a kind of displacement. Especially in the areas of sex and politics, the power of Highsmith's novels (and to a lesser extent her stories) derives from their not dealing with issues openly. Inevitably, when something is undiscussed, it assumes a greater power for its invisibility, its unknown quality. What, exactly, is the value of x in the equation? It might be very large. The problem presented by someone whose hole card we do not know is whether they are bluffing or not. Or, to put it specifically: To what extent does Highsmith really know what she is doing, and if she does not—well, we usually take points off for unconscious success, as when, without looking, we successfully toss a crumpled-up piece of paper into the wastebasket. "Let me see you do that again," we respond. Yet Highsmith did it again and again. It was not a fluke, and the question of intention seems irrelevant.

Notes and References

Preface

1. "*Strangers on a Train* had been published as 'A Harper Novel of Suspense'... so overnight I had become a 'suspense' writer, though *Strangers* in my mind was not categorized, and was simply a novel with an interesting story." Patricia Highsmith, afterword to *The Price of Salt* (Tallahassee, Fla.: The Naiad Press, 1993), n.p.; hereafter cited in the text as *Price*.

2. Highsmith's own description of suspense-writing problematics does not apply to much of her writing and rarely to the novels and stories I have chosen to discuss: "A suspense writer's problems are often concrete and have to do with things like the speed of the train, police procedure, the fatality of sleeping pills, limits of physical strength, and the reasonable boundary of police stupidity or intelligence." Patricia Highsmith, *Plotting and Writing Suspense Fiction* (Boston: The Writer, Inc., 1981), 85; hereafter cited in the text as *Plotting*.

3. Randy Kennedy, "Patricia Highsmith, Writer of Mysteries, Is Dead at 74," *New York Times,* 5 February 1995, A 47.

Chapter One

1. Christa Maerker, " 'Ich liebe Klarheit,' " *Horen* 38, no. 4 (1993): 149; hereafter cited in the text as Maerker.

2. This phrase is from a curriculum vitae Highsmith prepared for John Wakeman, perhaps for a reference work; hereafter cited in the text as Wakeman.

3. Noëlle Loriot, "Drei Tage mit Patricia Highsmith," in *Über Patricia Highsmith,* ed. Franz Cavigelli and Fritz Senn (Zurich: Diogenes, 1980), 35; hereafter cited in the text as Loriot.

4. Joan Dupont, "Criminal Pursuits," *New York Times Magazine,* 12 June 1988, 64; hereafter cited in the text as Dupont.

5. Ernest Mandel, *Delightful Murder: A Social History of the Crime Story* (Minneapolis: University of Minnesota Press, 1984), 88.

6. Jean-Paul Sartre, *Being and Nothingness,* trans. Hazel Barnes (New York: Washington Square Press, 1953), 523; hereafter cited in the text as Sartre.

7. Albert Camus, *The Myth of Sisyphus and Other Essays* (New York: Vintage, 1955), 38; hereafter cited in the text as Camus.

8. Fyodor Dostoyevsky, *Notes from Underground/The Double* (London: Penguin, 1972), 33.

9.   Kathleen Gregory Klein, "Patricia Highsmith," in *And Then There Were Nine . . . More Women of Mystery*, ed. Jane S. Bakerman (Bowling Green, Ohio: Bowling Green State University Popular Press, 1985), 196; hereafter cited in the text as Klein.

10.   Graham Greene, foreword to *Eleven*, by Patricia Highsmith (Harmondsworth: Penguin, 1972), 10; hereafter cited in the text as Greene.

11.   As Bernard Frechtman wrote in his introduction to the first English translation of a philosophical work by Sartre: "[P]eople have obscurely sensed that Sartre is occupied with a philosophy that is immediately involved in the peculiar confusions that beset this generation in all aspects of its civilization, the private as well as the public." Jean-Paul Sartre, *Existentialism* (New York: Philosophical Library, 1947), 2.

12.   The clearest example of the influence the proletarian moment in American literature had on Highsmith, a writer opposed to such a view of literature with every bone in her body, is the first chapter of *The Price of Salt*, a marvelous example of social realism.

13.   The cause of the riot is as follows: After a dog the prisoners have been keeping in the laundry is discovered and taken away to the local pound, the prisoners attempt to send a letter to a local newspaper to try to find a home for the dog. The letter is stopped by the prison authorities, and the sentences of all the men who signed it are extended by two months.

14.   Indeed, even after inheriting Dickie Greenleaf's money and marrying into money, Tom Ripley still has to work a bit in the Derwatt forgery project.

15.   As, for example, do Greg Wyncoop and Jenny Thierolf in *The Cry of the Owl* and Richard Semco and Therese Belivet in *The Price of Salt*. In a slight variation, Walter Stackhouse and Ellie Briess have sex once early in *The Blunderer*, desist for most of the novel, and then make love once more, just before Walter blunders to his death.

16.   Commodities are "a tangible good . . . resulting from the process of production." Graham Bannock, R. E. Baxter, and Evan Davis, eds., *The Penguin Dictionary of Economics* (Harmondsworth: The Penguin Group, 1972), 75; hereafter cited in the text as Bannock.

17.   A consumer good is "an economic good or commodity purchased by households for final consumption" (Bannock, 84).

18.   Theodor W. Adorno, *Notes to Literature,* vol. 2 (New York: Columbia University Press, 1991), 128. I have altered the second sentence of the translation slightly.

Chapter Two

1.   Patricia Highsmith, *Strangers on a Train* (Harmondsworth: Penguin, 1974), 30; hereafter cited in the text as *Strangers*.

2.   This was the question that Alfred Hitchcock and the scriptwriters (one of whom was Raymond Chandler) asked when they came to film the

novel. As Highsmith told an interviewer: "I remember that Alfred Hitchcock, when filming *Strangers on a Train* had difficulties—the scriptwriters also had problems. Hitchcock and the writers said: 'Why didn't Guy go to the police?' Yes, that's a good question." Holly-Jane Rahlens, "Patricia Highsmith im Gespräch mit Holly-Jane Rahlens," in *Über Patricia Highsmith,* ed. Franz Cavigelli and Fritz Senn (Zurich: Diogenes, 1980), 169–70; hereafter cited in the text as Rahlens.

   3.   In Highsmith's 1956 novel *The Blunderer,* Walter Stackhouse feels guilt—and is attracted to Melchior Kimmel, who has killed his own wife—because Stackhouse had *thought* about killing his wife, who, in fact, has committed suicide. Not for Highsmith's characters either Freud's dictum that one is not responsible for one's feelings, or Sartre's stricture that we can judge only from behavior.

   4.   As Klein writes: "Chief among Highsmith's deviations is her presentation of psychological motivation. . . . readers attempt to retrace the character's psychological state, mental attitude and reasoning patterns, which led to the decision to kill. Frequently there are none; or, none really matter. . . . all the clues either mislead or direct the reader to vacant lots" (Klein, 195).

   5.   Gide (influenced by Nietzsche) speculated in *Lafcadio's Adventures* "that evil actions—what are commonly called evil—may be just as gratuitous as good ones." And: " 'A crime without a motive;' went on Lafcadio, 'what a puzzle for the police!' " André Gide, *Lafcadio's Adventures,* trans. Dorothy Bussy (1925; reprint, New York: Vintage, 1953), 171, 186.

   6.   In this there are further resonances of Gide's Lafcadio. Lafcadio, too, lacks a father (though he has a series of substitutes), but, in contrast to Ripley, Gide explains Lafcadio's specific gifts through a detailed delineation of his formative years, his education, and so forth.

   7.   This refusal to provide the reader with such knowledge reflects Highsmith's personal views on the unimportance of such data: "The phrase 'poor schools' makes me laugh. I went to several [presumably not Barnard]. What counts is individual motivation. Ambition and drive count." Diana Cooper-Clark, "Patricia Highsmith—Interview," *The Armchair Detective* 14 (Fall 1981): 317; hereafter cited in the text as Cooper-Clark. But where do ambition and drive come from?

   8.   For instance, Tom (as do many of Highsmith's male protagonists) possesses superior taste: in art, clothes, food—just about everything. Where he has gained this is never even hinted at. (Later on, to be sure, Tom does read up on art.)

   9.   Patricia Highsmith, *The Talented Mr. Ripley* (Harmondsworth: Penguin, 1976), 52; hereafter cited in the text as *Ripley.*

   10.   Anthony Channell Hilfer, " 'Not Really Such a Monster': Highsmith's Ripley as Thriller Protagonist and Protean Man," *Midwest Quarterly: A Journal of Contemporary Thought* 25 (1984): 369.

11. Highsmith's comment on Ripley's sexuality is revealing: "He's got very little sexual drive, in my opinion. He has a sense of *aesthetics,* and he likes handsome boys and good looking men. . . . he likes good clothes." Patricia Highsmith, "A Talk with Patricia Highsmith," interview by Bettina Berch, Switzerland, 15 June 1984; hereafter cited in the text as Berch.

12. For an analysis of Dickie, as well as for an interpretation that focuses on Tom's search for identity, see Erlene Hubly, "A Portrait of the Artist: The Novels of Patricia Highsmith," *Clues* 5 (1984): 127.

Chapter Three

1. Anthony Boucher, review of *Deep Water,* by Patricia Highsmith, *New York Times,* 6 October 1957, 34.

2. Patricia Highsmith, *Deep Water* (Harmondsworth: Penguin, 1974), 22; hereafter cited in the text as *Deep.*

3. I think "relationships," rather than "affairs," might better characterize Melinda's relations with men in the novel, with one exception. Otherwise, Melinda denies that her relationships are sexual, and we have only circumstantial evidence and Vic's own feelings about her relationships as evidence that her denials are untrue. (The novel is, almost without exception, told from Vic's point of view.) In her last relationship with Anthony Cameron, she comes close to acknowledging its sexual nature by admitting that she is planning to leave with Cameron and will ask Vic for a divorce. It should also be noted that Vic has lost sexual interest in Melinda and reacts not so much against her sexual infidelity as against the openness with which she socializes with her male friends and against their inevitable "inferiority" as object choices. Highsmith, on the other hand, contends that Melinda does have a number of affairs, although she exaggerates their frequency: "And then Melinda, who was Vic's wife, was always flirting and having two or three lovers" (Cooper-Clark, 318).

4. That psyche is adumbrated in a quotation from Dostoyevsky's *The Possessed* prefaced to the novel: "There is no better dodge than one own's character, because no one believes in it" (*Deep,* 6). Although the quotation is from Peter Verkhovensky, the somewhat bizarre head of a revolutionary cell operating in a small provincial Russian city of the late 1860s, it is Nicolai Stavrogin whom Vic Van Allen more closely resembles. Both Stavrogin and Vic behave as if they are superior to the ordinary laws of social life and engage in outlandish behavior (such as Vic's "confessing" to a murder he has not committed). But in the end Stavrogin's behavior, though in part a function of the "demon of irony" that "torments" him, serves political motives. Although Highsmith, in developing that demon into Vic's quasi-schizophrenic distance from his own emotions, has deprived it—on the surface—of any political content, the several areas in which *Deep Water* converges with Dostoyevsky's most overtly political novel suggest that Highsmith is beginning to place individual issues in a social context. The novels converge not only in their exploration of issues such as choice

and the absurd but also in their narrowly circumscribed locales, in which public opinion and society in general play an important role. Fyodor Dostoyevsky, *The Devils* (Harmondsworth: Penguin, 1953), 197.

5. Thomas Sutcliffe, "Graphs of Innocence and Guilt," *TLS*, 2 October 1981, 1118; hereafter cited in the text as Sutcliffe.

6. Highsmith's comment in an interview, therefore, should not surprise us: "My good friends tell me, 'Pat, your knowledge of human nature is miserable. Strange, that you're actually a writer' " (Maerker, 148).

7. With the exception of Therese Belivet, in *The Price of Salt* (1952), one of the most successful characterizations in any of Highsmith's fiction. I discuss *The Price of Salt* in chapter 6 in the context of the gay fiction.

8. Odette L'Henry Evans, "A Feminist Approach to Patricia Highsmith's Fiction," in *American Horror Fiction: From Brockden Brown to Stephen King*, ed. Brian Docherty (New York: St. Martin's Press, 1990), 114; hereafter cited in the text as Evans.

9. In the Richard Yates's *Revolutionary Road* (1961) and Bruce Jay Friedman's *Stern* (1962), the role of the house is different than in Highsmith's novel, but central. In Yates, the suburban house represents a sacrifice of youthful ideals, and in Friedman the anxiety of second-generation immigrant success in WASP America.

10. The term brings to mind Sartre's discussion of the same term in *Being and Nothingness*, where he "use[s] the term *situation* for the contingency of freedom" (Sartre, 626). By this he means that our free choice causes certain conditions to become problematic for us. Here, David's choice to continue his courtship of Annabelle after her marriage to Gerald creates his situation. It is proof of his freedom.

11. Patricia Highsmith, *This Sweet Sickness* (Harmondsworth: Penguin, 1982), 22; hereafter cited in the text as *Sweet*.

12. Positional goods are "goods that are necessarily scarce and whose scarcity cannot be increased by increased productivity" (Bannock, 33). An example would be David Kelsey's "manuscript page of a Beethoven theme."

13. See, for example, the thoughtful review by Francis Wyndham, *New Statesman*, 31 May 1963. The review is one of the better summaries of Highsmith's career to that date.

14. Patricia Highsmith, *The Cry of the Owl* (Harmondsworth: Penguin, 1973), 9; hereafter cited in the text as *Cry*.

15. Beate Finke, *Erzählsituationen und Figurenperspektiven im Detektivroman* (Amsterdam: B. R. Grüner, 1983), 238; hereafter cited in the text as Finke.

16. In fact, as a result of Robert's relative rationality, Finke saw the novel as the "comparatively most optimistic" of Highsmith's works (Finke, 242).

17. For a detailed description of Highsmith's uses of point of view as an aid to characterization in *The Cry of the Owl*, see Finke, 232–38.

18. At first, these instances involve only people who are peripheral to Robert, neighbors or casual acquaintances, and the police. But as the novel pro-

gresses and Greg continues to remain in hiding, those closer to Robert also begin to lose faith in him. The most striking, and pathetic, case is Jenny herself. She comes to believe that Robert did kill Greg and, although she is still in love with Robert, feels the only solution is death. She commits suicide by taking a bottle of sleeping pills *and* slitting her wrists, leaving a note that casts Robert in an unenviable light.

19. Although I do not discuss it in detail, Highsmith's next novel, *The Glass Cell* (1964), assumes importance in this respect. Although the novel deals with the unjust conviction and imprisonment of its protagonist on embezzlement charges, Highsmith, in her portrayal of the prison population, represented for the first time individuals who become involved in a cause that is greater than themselves. The representation is in some ways trivialized, but the fact remains that in this novel, for the first time, she depicted individuals joining together to better their collective condition, the suggestion of a political moment.

Chapter Four

1. By "marked" I mean that it diverges from traditional fiction in incorporating elements of suspense fiction.

2. This was Terrence Rafferty's judgment in "Fear and Trembling," *New Yorker,* 1 January 1988, 74–76; hereafter cited in the text as Rafferty. An anonymous contemporary reviewer, though questioning the novel's overall value ("at the end, though, it hardly seems to have been worthwhile"), acknowledged that it was "an accomplished book, with a high degree of virtuosity, the work of a deft, original writer with much insight into people and places." "Resilient Unease," *TLS,* 20 March 1969, 287; hereafter cited in the text as "Resilient Unease."

3. The element of uprootedness is suggested on the novel's second page when Ingham is disoriented by a conversation he overhears: "Arabic would obviously have to be memorized, because it bore no relation to anything he knew." Ingham's mild alienation from society is indicated in the title of his two novels: *The Power of Negative Thinking* and *The Gathering Swine.* Patricia Highsmith, *The Tremor of Forgery* (New York: Atlantic Monthly Press, 1988), 2; hereafter cited in the text as *Tremor.*

4. More recently, in Edward Said's *Culture and Imperialism* (1993), *The Stranger'*s shelf life has been extended by drawing it into discussions of postcoloniality. By virtue of the context in which she places the events (the Six Days' War, the Vietnam War), Highsmith gives Camus's novel a Saidian reading *avant la lettre.*

5. The acts reflect the different ideologies of the two imperialist powers. Although Meurseault has murdered a native, the native is a colonized subject and thus formally (i.e., legally) of less worth than the European colonist. That Western critics could see the murder as "gratuitous," that is, meaningless,

underlines this. But Highsmith, as the product of a different ideology, is constrained in ways that Camus was not. For all her debt to French existentialism and the absurd, she could not, I think, as an American whose ideological formation occurred in the 1930s and 1940s, have written of the "gratuitous" murder of a native by an American. Hence, the doubt surrounding the murder of the Arab and Ingham's unwillingness to admit his complicity do not just provide examples of Sartrean bad faith but rather mirror the United States' unwillingness to see itself as engaged in an imperialist act in Vietnam (the subject of the political discussions between Ingham and Adams). Last, one might suggest that the mediation between Ingham and the object of his violence mirrors an oft-noted aspect of the Vietnam War: American soldiers rarely saw their enemy because they were either bombing them from planes thousands of feet above, or off the shore shelling them from battleships, or prevented by the dense foliage of the jungle. But the possible murder of an Arab by an American in the late 1960s, at the height of America's involvement in Vietnam, is a different story on more than this account. First of all, whatever the facts "on the ground" have been, America's ideology has always been that of a noncolonial power. Thus Ingham's possible murder, committed in self-defense and not with the primary aim of killing, quite effectively mirrors the "cover" for the American involvement in Vietnam: The United States was there not out of evil, imperialist motives but in self-defense (the "domino theory"), the justification being that our vital interests as a nation were threatened (a rationalization that might justifiably suggest "the absurd").

6. Rafferty saw this inconsequentiality as the novel's "irresolution" (Rafferty, 75), and the *TLS* reviewer saw it as Ingham's being "perhaps too resilient for the kind of ordeal to which he is subjected" ("Resilient Unease," 287).

7. In opposition to Jefferson, Hamilton felt that in its foreign relations, the United States could engage in the sometimes cynical manipulations practiced by European nations without its own domestic democracy being affected.

8. That is, the absolutely neutral quality that the French critic Roland Barthes saw in the prose of a novel such as Camus's *The Stranger.*

9. The book's initial reviewers did not generally acknowledge its socioeconomic dimensions. Representative reviews in *The New Statesman* (28 April 1972, 571), *TLS* (12 May 1972, 537), and the *New York Times Book Review* (3 September 1972, 22) all view the novel as another study in the psychopathic personality. This is all the odder in that Kenneth Rowajinski dies well before the halfway point of the novel.

10. This is of more significance in *A Dog's Ransom* because with the rise of the youth countercultures, slang began to play a more important part as a marker of cultural differences, and Highsmith's absence from the American scene placed her at a disadvantage. Yet this failure allows us to see both the

attempts the novel makes to come to grips with the social and where it fails. Oddly, the *New York Times* reviewer sensed "a good ear for dialogue" (22), which strikes me as another indication of the establishment's distance from the social changes occurring.

11.   "The sixties" (as opposed to the strictly temporal phrase "the 1960s") is here used as a metonym for the various social changes associated with the decade: the civil rights movement (which the novel does not directly address), the movement against the Vietnam War, the youth and countercultural movements, and feminism.

12.   Patricia Highsmith, *A Dog's Ransom* (Harmondsworth: Penguin, 1975), 47; hereafter cited in the text as *Dog's.*

13.   I would hazard the guess that somewhere affecting Highsmith in her creation of this character was the historical figure of George Metesky, the so-called Mad Bomber of mid-1950s New York City, who was motivated by a work-related grudge against his former employer, Con Edison.

14.   Hypo-descent is the tendency to assign someone of mixed ancestry the ethnicity or role of the lower-status ancestor.

15.   For example, Highsmith changed the phrase "Negro boy" to "black man" in the revised printing in 1993 of her 1952 novel *The Price of Salt.* The phrases occur on p. 182 of both editions.

16.   The term *ressentiment* derives from Nietzsche and denotes the group resentment of an inferior social group toward the superior group, "the *ressentiment* of natures that are denied the true reaction, that of deeds, and compensate themselves with an imaginary revenge." Friedrich Nietzsche, *Genealogy of Morals,* in Walter Kaufmann, ed., *Basic Writings of Nietzsche* (New York: Modern Library, 1968), p. 472.

17.   Reference might be made here to Highsmith's short story "The Network" (1976), which also depicts a middle-class Manhattan milieu exposed to a variety of unsettling—even threatening—forces. The story is collected in *Slowly, Slowly in the Wind.*

18.   The civil rights movement, something we would expect to find in any treatment of the decade, is almost wholly absent from the novel, appearing only in such peripheral moments as Clarence's conservative response to affirmative action (an important issue in "The Network," too). One reason is the displacement of race through the ethnic markers (Polish and Italian).

19.   A further indication of Highsmith's problem in confronting the issue of Vietnam is that Clarence himself, though drafted into the army at the height of the War, has somehow "escaped" Vietnam. This possible, though unlikely, outcome suggests the author's inability to engage the issue.

20.   As the critic Teresa Ebert points out, the role of the police in detective fiction is to restore the status quo ante of patriarchal capitalist society: "Detective fictions are narratives of crisis in patriarchy," and "The mystery or crime to be solved . . . initiates or marks a fundamental crisis of legitimation in patriarchy." The large part the police play in *A Dog's Ransom* indicates the criti-

cal nature of the threats, whereas the dog's death almost before the novel begins suggests the impossibility of restoring the status quo. Although crimes had been committed in Highsmith's earlier novels, those crimes did not fundamentally threaten society. For example, in *The Talented Mr. Ripley,* the replacement of Dickie Greenleaf by Tom Ripley merely enacts a "circulation of elites," to use the sociologist Vilfredo Pareto's phrase; the basic social structure remains unchanged. Indeed, much of the novel concerns Tom's trying to become Dickie. Hence, the criminal justice system plays only a minor role. Teresa Ebert, "Detecting the Phallus: Authority, Ideology, and the Production of Patriarchal Agents in Detective Fiction," *Rethinking Marxism* 5, no. 3 (Fall 1992): 6.

21.   Clearly the novel is ambivalent in how it regards the state as this suturing agent. If it were not, then the police would have been the ones to effect Rowajinski's removal. Yet the fact that they could not do this reveals the novel's ambivalence. Also, that problems might be solved socially—as opposed to individually—was something that went against the grain of the author's deepest convictions. Hence, the devolution upon Clarence to right the wrong.

22.   Simone de Beauvoir's *The Second Sex,* first published in English in 1953, is perhaps the most well-known theoretical-historical precursor to the women's movement, which began a decade after the book's publication. Highsmith refers to Beauvoir's book in a discussion of *Edith's Diary* (Loriot, 44).

23.   Before *Edith's Diary,* the most extended treatment of such things occurred through the figure of Madame Annette in the later Ripley novels. In these books, however, the topic was constructed differently. Madame Annette is a worker who delights in doing her job and in doing it well, in part because her relationship to Tom Ripley has something of a personal (indeed, almost feudal) quality to it. Moreover, in the Ripley novels, purchases of food and clothing are carefully calculated pleasures in themselves. In particular, food is shopped for and prepared by Madame Annette. Such things as the choice of a wine or the purchase of a gift are significant in the psychological economy of the individual, but they are luxuries; in fact, it is their unnecessary quality that provides much of their appeal, as one more area in which Tom Ripley might pleasurably exercise his good taste. Their overall signification in the novels derives from the fact that they represent a choice on the part of the individual. If the element of necessity was present, the novels would be very different. The Ripleys swim in a sea of tasteful upscale commodities. The superfluousness of the material objects with which they are surrounded serves to define them.

24.   Patricia Highsmith, *Edith's Diary* (Harmondsworth: Penguin, 1980), 33–34; hereafter cited in the text as *Diary.*

25.   In another interview, Highsmith said she was aiming at "an absolute realism, every moment in the daily routine of a housewife. Can't they see that such a life is stiflingly dull to the point of anxiety?" she asked, referring to people who had criticized her manuscript as being "flat, heavy and without brio" (Loriot, 34–35).

26.   Simone de Beauvoir, *The Second Sex* (New York: Vintage, 1974), 503.

27. "But the main fault of the book is really its ambition, its desire to be a portrait of Our Times." Michael Wood, "A Heavy Legacy," *The New York Review of Books,* 15 October 1977, 32; hereafter cited in the text as Wood.

28. Kathleen Gregory Klein presents as convincing a view as I have seen for Edith's not being insane. In general, Klein's reading of the novel is the most nuanced I have read and the best presentation of it as a feminist book, or as she puts it, "this covertly feminist novel" (Klein, 185).

29. The significance of Edith's refusal of independent financial aid is all the more striking in the context of the long line of Highsmith's protagonists who receive such aid. It is another indication of the unusual place *Edith's Diary* occupies in Highsmith's oeuvre.

30. ˙ She told Rahlens that she found the stories "pro-women's lib—they speak for the emancipation of the woman" (166). Yet the *TLS* reviewer seemed more on the mark when he wrote that "It would be wrong to read these stories as indirectly feminist satires on dependency, because the real center of their inspiration is the delight which Patricia Highsmith everywhere shows for the brutal ways in which these women are . . . murdered." Tom Paulin, "Mortem Virumque Cano," *TLS,* 25 November 1977, 744.

31. One of the most striking examples of such male identification occurs in *The Cry of the Owl* when Jenny Thierolf tells the "prowling" David Forester that in her opinion, the worst conceivable crime was "to accuse somebody falsely of rape" (22).

32. Joan Dupont, "The Poet of Apprehension: Patricia Highsmith's Furtive Generosities," *Village Voice,* 30 May 1995, 28.

33. There is a link here between her conservatism in this area with other aspects of her weltanshauung. She refuses to see anything in terms of units larger than the individual. The world, for Highsmith, consists of individuals. Classes, even interest groups, such as those that have come to characterize identity politics, do not exist in any meaningful way in her fiction. Hence the difficulty in feeling solidarity with women generally.

Chapter Five

1. Compare its characterization as a "classic" and "one of the two or three all time best in the field" (i.e., of lesbian novels). Barbara Grier, *Lesbiana: Book Reviews from the Ladder, 1966–1972* (Tallahassee, Fla.: The Naiad Press, 1976), 162.

2. Patricia Highsmith, *The Price of Salt* (Tallahassee, Fla.: The Naiad Press, 1993), 279. One cannot help thinking, however, that in the early 1950s, during the height of the McCarthy purges of various institutions on "moral" as well as political grounds, an unwillingness to be seen as a lesbian writer may also have caused Highsmith to resort to a pseudonym.

3. One recalls other embodiments of this drive in her fiction, especially David Kelsey's passion, in *This Sweet Sickness,* for creating a controlled space.

What alters this dynamic in *The Price of Salt* is the change in the balance of power between the lovers.

4. On visiting Richard's (her boyfriend) home, Therese muses to herself about his bedroom: "She loved the room—because it stayed the same and stayed in the same place" (*Price,* 86). Although a room's furnishings may change, it seems odd to feel relief that the room is in the same place.

5. Another attempt to deny the family is made when Therese tells Carol that both her parents are dead, although her mother is alive.

6. A good example of this "transvaluation of values" occurs toward the end of the novel in an odd juxtaposition of people and things. After Carol has flown back to New Jersey to handle her divorce, Therese is alone in Sioux Falls and very much feeling Carol's absence:

> There were simply the mornings, mornings anywhere, when she could lift her head from a pillow and see Carol's face, and know that the day was theirs and that nothing would separate them.
>
> And there was the beautiful thing, transfixing the heart and the eyes at once, in the dark window of an antique shop in a street where she had never been. Therese stared at it feeling it quench some forgotten and nameless thirst inside her. *(Price, 238)*

The "beautiful thing" is a tiny candlestick holder that Therese buys for Carol.

7. Quoting other sexual descriptions in the novel, some reviewers did not feel this was one of the novel's achievements. See Caroline Moore, "Confessions of a Justified Lover," *The Spectator,* 13 October 1990, 33, and Susannah Clapp, "Lovers on a Train," *London Review of Books,* 10 January 1991, 19.

8. Highsmith notes in her afterword that the happy ending brought her many approving letters. She received "envelopes of ten and fifteen letters a couple of times a week for months on end" (*Price,* 279). When the novel was issued in paperback in 1953, it sold nearly 1,000,000 copies. Julie Abraham, however, argues that in much lesbian fiction, including *The Price of Salt,* "the progress of the lesbian relationship is shaped in detail by its relationship to the heterosexual plot" and that lesbian novels "focus their representations of lesbianism on sex/romance," thus "limit[ing] female subjects to the plot of romance." Indeed, the novel's " 'happy ending' only reinscribes the romance as the focus of representations of lesbianism." Julie Abraham, *Are Girls Necessary? Lesbian Writing and Modern Histories* (New York: Routledge, 1996), 12.

9. The most telling example of the utilitarian value of Jack's artistic skill is a chance sketch he makes early in the novel, which proves important in finding Elsie's murderer.

10. Patricia Highsmith, *Found in the Street* (New York: Atlantic Monthly Press, 1989), 22; hereafter cited in the text as *Found.*

11. Although my emphasis on the importance that objectification plays in Highsmith's work may strike the reader as tendentious, I do not think this

aspect can be overstressed. It has definite effects on her prose style and contributes to the alienating effect that is an important aspect of her novels. Here it is shown in the adjectival clause "which she'd taken from the house to wear." The clause produces two specific effects. First, devoting such a substantial clause to the noun emphasizes that object. Second, it is a marked, and even awkward, locution for the more expected "she was wearing" or "she had on." It shifts part of the reason for Natalia's appeal to her decisiveness ("she had taken") vis-à-vis the object.

12. Patricia Highsmith, *Small g: A Summer Idyll* (London: Bloomsbury, 1995), 177; hereafter cited in the text as *g*.

13. Knopf rejected the novel. Their editor is quoted as saying, "Were I to have published that book it would have conceivably done harm to what small strides we made toward establishing her. It's a very sweet and baffling book. In the best of all possible worlds it would be published as a young adult title, but the lunatic right-wing fringe that's running this country wouldn't have that. I imagine some probably crass American publisher will do it." Joan Dupont, "The Poet of Apprehension," *Village Voice,* 30 May 1995, 29. Dupont notes that only 4,000 copies of *Found in the Street* were sold in the United States. On the other hand, *Small g* had sold 45,800 copies in French translation within a few months of its publication.

Chapter Six

1. Patricia Highsmith, "The Network," in *Slowly, Slowly in the Wind* (Harmondsworth: Penguin, 1982), 16; hereafter cited in the text as *Slowly*.

2. The overdetermined quality is here revealed in two ways. First, "spicks" is redundant because it is slang for Puerto Ricans; second, the misspelling of the word using the "k" reveals the author's distance from the milieu she is attempting to describe and hence goes some way toward undercutting the description as authentic, that is, realistic. There is a similar effect in the misuse of the word "diddled" in the first passage quoted. Lest I be thought heavy-handed in my characterizing the story as mildly racist, it should be noted that Highsmith's identification with her characters seems strong (if not complete), and there is no evidence of irony at any point in the story.

3. Often enough, what clues the reader in to the "failed" realism of a Highsmith text is a small detail, as here the suggestion that there is such a position as "subway guard." There are transit policemen, but "subway guard" is "off" enough to indicate that we are not in the realm of the typical, which social realism prizes as its raison d'être.

4. Karl Marx, *Capital: A Critique of Political Economy,* vol. 1 of *The Process of Capitalist Production* (New York: International Publishers, 1967), 71–72; hereafter cited in the text as Marx.

5. Patricia Highsmith, "The Terrors of Basket-Weaving," in *The Black House* (Harmondsworth: Penguin, 1982), 49; hereafter cited in the text as *Black*.

6. Diane's terror at her possible bond with her ancestors nicely underlines another aspect of Marx's analysis of the commodity form: the "mystery" of the commodity form derived from the fact that "the sum total of their own labor is presented as a social relation, existing not between themselves, but between the products of their labor" (Marx, 72). Diane has become so alienated that she fears the reverse, the social relations of people, that is, her relations to her ancestors.

7. When groups exist in Highsmith, they are often of an us-against-them nature, as in "The Network" and also in "Not One of Us" (in *The Black House*), a story in which a group of middle-class Manhattanites unite to drive to drink and eventually death a member of their small social circle whom they have decided (because he bores them) is not one of them.

8. Highsmith turns Sartre, as well as Marx, on his head. Compare the following passage from *Being and Nothingness,* where Sartre is analyzing the phenomenon of "possession": "This cane which I have cut from the branch is also destined to belong to me in this double relation: first as an object for everyday use, which is at my disposition and which I possess as I possess my clothes or my books, and second as my own work. Thus people who like to surround themselves with everyday objects which they themselves have made, are enjoying subtleties of appropriation" (Sartre, 737). Diane, and many of Highsmith's characters, desire no such subtlety in their various appropriations.

9. Patricia Highsmith, "A Clock Ticks at Christmas," *Mermaids on the Golf Course* (Harmondsworth: Penguin, 1986), 91; hereafter cited in the text as *Golf.*

10. This has given rise to a Lacanian reading by Slavoj Zizek that produces interesting (though to my mind narrow) interpretations. Using Lacan's concept of "the Imaginary," a place not of needs or demands but rather of desire (something that does not exist), Zizek suggests that Highsmith's story "perfectly exemplifies the way fantasy space functions as an empty surface, as a kind of screen for the projection of desires." He bases his interpretation of the story on the supposition that men's boasts are fantasy. To the central enigma—why are the men so upset by Timothy's denial of significance to the black house?— Zizek writes: "We can grasp their resentment by remarking the difference between reality and the 'other scene' of the fantasy space: the 'black house' was forbidden to the men because it functioned as an empty space wherein they could project their empty desires, their distorted memories; by publicly stating that the 'black house' was nothing but an old ruin, the young intruder reduced their fantasy space to everyday, common reality. He annulled the difference between reality and fantasy space, depriving the men of the place in which they were able to articulate their desires." Although Zizek's is an intriguing interpretation, it does not account for the murder of the young man, which is not portrayed as being in doubt. Such an interpretation deals with desire but ignores its social mediations. Slavoj Zizek, *Looking Awry: An Introduction to*

Jacques Lacan through Popular Culture (Cambridge: MIT Press, 1991), 8, 9. In addition to "The Black House," Zizek discusses "The Mysterious Cemetery," "The Button," "The Stuff of Madness," and "The Pond."

11.   That the house cannot be the scene of the family is underlined at the beginning of the story when the question of who owns the house is discussed. It is suggested that the house is jointly owned by two cousins. A little later, when Tim asks his uncle, a lawyer, why the house is not being maintained, he is told: "Because legally speaking no one's got the right to touch the property till the case is settled" (*Black*, 233).

12.   Judith Fetterly, *The Resisting Reader: A Feminist Approach to American Literature* (Bloomington: Indiana University Press, 1978), 3.

Selected Bibliography

PRIMARY SOURCES

Novels

The Blunderer. New York: Coward-McCann, 1954.
The Boy Who Followed Ripley. London: William Heinemann, 1980.
The Cry of the Owl. New York: Harper and Row, 1962.
Deep Water. New York: Harper and Row, 1957.
A Dog's Ransom. Alfred A. Knopf, 1972.
Edith's Diary. New York: Simon and Schuster, 1977.
Found in the Street. London: William Heinemann, 1986.
A Game for the Living. New York: Harper and Row, 1958.
The Glass Cell. New York: Doubleday, 1964.
People Who Knock on the Door. London: William Heinemann, 1983.
The Price of Salt. New York: Coward-McCann, 1952.
Ripley's Game. London: William Heinemann, 1974.
Ripley under Ground. New York: Doubleday, 1970.
Ripley under Water. New York: Alfred A. Knopf, 1992.
Small g: A Summer Idyll. London: Bloomsbury, 1995.
Strangers on a Train. New York: Harper and Brothers, 1950.
A Suspension of Mercy. New York: Doubleday, 1965.
The Talented Mr. Ripley. New York: Coward-McCann, 1955.
This Sweet Sickness. New York: Harper and Row, 1960.
Those Who Walk Away. New York: Doubleday, 1967.
The Tremor of Forgery. New York: Doubleday, 1969.
The Two Faces of January. New York: Doubleday, 1964.

Short Story Collections

The Animal-Lover's Book of Beastly Murder. London: William Heinemann, 1975.
The Black House. London: William Heinemann, 1981.
Eleven. London: William Heinemann, 1970.
Little Tales of Misogyny. London: William Heinemann, 1977.
Mermaids on the Golf Course. London: William Heinemann, 1985.
Slowly, Slowy in the Wind. London: William Heinemann, 1979.
Tales of Natural and Unnatural Catastrophes. London: Bloomsbury, 1987.

Nonfiction

Plotting and Writing Suspense Fiction. Boston: The Writer, 1981.

Interviews

Berch, Bettina. "A Talk with Patricia Highsmith." Unpublished interview. Switzerland, 15 June 1984.

Cooper-Clark, Diana. "Patricia Highsmith—Interview." *The Armchair Detective* 14 (Fall 1981): 313–20.

Dupont, Joan. "Criminal Pursuits." *New York Times Magazine,* 12 June 1988, 61–66.

Loriot, Noëlle. "Drei Tage mit Patricia Highsmith." In *Über Patricia Highsmith,* edited by Franz Cavigelli and Fritz Senn. Zürich: Diogenes, 1980.

Maerker, Christa. " 'Ich liebe Klarheit. . . .' " *Horen* 38, no. 4 (1993): 146–53.

Rahlens, Holly-Jane. "Patricia Highsmith im Gespräch mit Holly-Jane Rahlens." In *Über Patricia Highsmith,* edited by Franz Cavigelli and Fritz Senn. Zürich: Diogenes, 1980.

SECONDARY SOURCES

As of 1 January 1996, no books, monographs, or dissertations dealing exclusively with Highsmith's work had been published. There are several good articles and reviews in English and German and several discussions of her work in larger contexts. I list what I think is the most useful material. In addition the collection of essays and interviews edited by Senn and Cavigelli has an excellent bibliography of German and English sources up to 1980.

Abraham, July. *Are Girls Necessary? Lesbian Writing and Modern Histories.* New York: Routledge, 1996.

Boucher, Anthony. Review of *Deep Water. New York Times Book Review,* 6 October 1957, C 12.

Brophy, Brigid. "Highsmith." Review of *A Suspension of Mercy* and *The Cry of the Owl.* In *Don't Never Forget,* by Brigid Brophy. New York: Holt, Rinehart and Winston, 1966.

Clapp, Susannah. "Lovers on a Train." Review of *Carol* [*The Price of Salt*]. *London Review of Books,* 10 January 1991, 19.

Borgmeier, Raimund. "Patricia Highsmith—Giving Crime Writing a Good Name." *Anglistik and Englischunterricht* 37 (1989): 43–63.

Duncker, Michael. *Beeinflussung und Steuerung des Lesers in der englischsprachigen Detektiv- und Kriminalliteratur: eine vergleichende Untersuchung zur Beziehung Autor—Text—Leser in Werken von Doyle, Christie und Highsmith.* Frankfurt: Peter Lang, 1991.

Evans, Odette L'Henry. "A Feminist Approach to Patricia Highsmith's Fiction." In *American Horror Fiction: From Brockden Brown to Stephen King,* edited by Brian Doherty. New York: St. Martin's Press, 1990.

Finke, Beate. *Erzählsituationen und Figurenperspektiven im Detektivroman.* Amsterdam: B. R. Grüner, 1983.

Greene, Graham. Foreword to *Eleven,* by Patricia Highsmith. Harmondsworth: Penguin, 1972.

Handke, Peter. "Die privaten Weltkriege der Patricia Highsmith." In *Das Ende des Flanierens,* by Peter Handke. Frankfurt: Suhrkamp, 1980. (This is also collected in Cavigelli and Senn, *Über Patricia Highsmith.*)

Hilfer, Anthony Channell. " 'Not Really Such a Monster': Highsmith's Ripley as Thriller Protagonist and Protean Man." *Midwest Quarterly: A Journal of Contemporary Thought* 25 (1984): 361–74.

Hubly, Erlene. "A Portrait of the Artist: The Novels of Patricia Highsmith." *Clues* 5 (1984): 115–30.

Klein, Kathleen Gregory. "Patricia Highsmith." In *And Then There Were Nine . . . More Women of Mystery,* edited by Jane S. Bakerman. Bowling Green, Ohio: Bowling Green State University Popular Press, 1985.

Moore, Caroline. "Confessions of a Justified Lover." Review of *Carol* [*The Price of Salt*]. *The Spectator,* 13 October 1990, 33.

Rafferty, Terrence. "Fear and Trembling." *New Yorker,* 1 January 1988, 74–76.

"Resilient Unease." Review of *The Tremor of Forgery. TLS,* 20 March 1969, 287.

Sutcliffe, Thomas. "Graphs of Innocence and Guilt." Review of *The Black House. TLS,* 2 October 1981, 1118.

Wood, Michael. "A Heavy Legacy." Review of *Edith's Diary. The New York Review of Books,* 15 October 1977, 32.

Wyndham, Francis. "Miss Highsmith." Review of *The Cry of the Owl. New Statesman,* 31 May 1963, 833–34.

Zizek, Slavoj. *Looking Awry: An Introduction to Jacques Lacan through Popular Culture.* Cambridge: MIT Press, 1991.

Index

The Author

Russell Harrison was educated at City College (CUNY), SUNY Binghamton, and SUNY Buffalo. The author of *Against the American Dream: Essays on Charles Bukowski* (Black Sparrow Press, 1994), he is Fulbright Lecturer in American literature at Minsk State Linguistic University in Minsk, Belarus, during the 1996–1997 academic year.

The Editor

Frank Day is a professor of English and head of the English Department at Clemson University. He is the author of *Sir William Empson: An Annotated Bibliography* (1984) and *Arthur Koestler: A Guide to Research* (1985). He was a Fulbright lecturer in American literature in Romania (1980–1981) and in Bangladesh (1986–1987).